India's Global Challenge
Growth and Leadership in the 21st Century

edited by Ugo Tramballi and Nicola Missaglia

ISPI

© 2019 Ledizioni LediPublishing
Via Alamanni, 11 – 20141 Milano – Italy
www.ledizioni.it
info@ledizioni.it

INDIA'S GLOBAL CHALLENGE. GROWTH AND LEADERSHIP IN THE 21ST
CENTURY
Edited by Ugo Tramballi and Nicola Missaglia
First edition: June 2019

The opinions expressed herein are strictly personal and do not necessarily reflect the position of ISPI.

Cover image created by Diana Orefice

Print ISBN   9788855260060
ePub ISBN   9788855260084
Pdf ISBN   9788855260107
DOI   10.14672/55260060

ISPI. Via Clerici, 5
20121, Milan
www.ispionline.it

Catalogue and reprints information: www.ledizioni.it

Table of Contents

Introduction

"India stands tall as a space power!" tweeted Prime Minister Narendra Modi just weeks before securing a second, spectacular landslide win in India's general election in Spring 2019 by an even bigger margin than many had expected. Minutes earlier, he had announced in a rare televised speech that India had just succeeded in shooting down one of its own satellites in low-Earth orbit with a ballistic ground-to-space rocket. Modi also added that the effort had been a fully "indigenous" one, accomplished entirely by Indians.

Blasting apart a satellite that orbits the globe at 17,000 mph, analysts say, represents a technological breakthrough, one that puts India in the small club of nations with such a capability, along with the United States, China, and Russia. The event established the country as a military space power and confirmed a significant military advance in an area where China want to be a dominant power. "Now, it's India's turn", Prime Minister Modi assured the country in a speech arguing for a bigger role for it on the world stage, delivered in Kuala Lumpur back in 2015, one year after his Bharatiya Janata Party stormed to victory in a landslide general election.

India's explosive economic growth over the last three decades has rapidly made it one of the world's major emerging powers. Today, the country is at a tipping point both in terms of economic growth and in terms of the opportunities available to its people, who now number far more than one billion. India is the world's sixth largest economy, with a GDP that has soared from US$270 billion in 1991 to US$2.6 trillion in 2017, and has a projected 2019 GDP growth rate of almost 7.5%, as the country continues – and will continue – to be a leading engine of world economic growth. India is also the world's largest democracy – which China is not – and will soon become the world's most populous nation, with almost 1.35 billion Indians in thousands of large (and growing) cities, as well as small towns and villages. Looking ahead to 2030, according to World Economic Forum estimates, India will still be a relatively young nation with an average age of 31 years (compared to 40 in the US and 42 in China), and will add more working-age citizens to the world's workforce than any other country.

The sheer scale of these numbers means that, whether willing or not, India's actions will have a major global impact in the medium and longer term. Economic growth has transformed it from a bit player on the international stage to a leading actor. Yet there is a widespread feeling throughout the country that India – now ages away from the land of beggars and gurus portrayed until recently in the Western media – has not yet been given its due on the global stage, despite its size, its achievements and its vibrant democracy. It is no accident that governments in New Delhi have long been urging the international community to recognise India's rise with a greater global voice at the high table of world powers, and a greater role in global institutions such as the United Nations Security Council. Pressure from India to reform twentieth-century organisations such as the IMF and the World Bank so as to take the growing weight and changing interests of emerging economies into account is another demonstration of the country's growing confidence.

India is not a revisionist power, though: while clearly becoming less reticent about its global ambitions, New Delhi has reaffirmed its commitment to multilateralism – in the form of the Paris Climate Agreement, for instance, where it stood by its responsibilities just as the United States chose to withdraw. India today also plays a more prominent leadership role as a vocal member of global institutions such as the World Trade

Organization and the Group of Twenty (G20). "India stands for a democratic and rules-based international order", said its External Affairs Minister, Sushma Swaraj, in a public speech in early 2019. "While the prosperity and security of Indians, both at home and abroad, is of paramount importance", she added, "self-interest alone does not propel us". This kind of commitment is no small feat at a time when the liberal democratic world order and its multilateral institutions are under threat from a growing number of actors including, alas, their principal architect.

Despite these times of global uncertainty, India is undeniably on the path to becoming a regional and global power. What kind of global power does it want to be? Its commitments have made this fairly clear, although only time will tell whether it will be able to put those commitments into practice in its actions, legislation and response to change.

One thing, however, is sure: no success comes without challenges; and for India challenges abound, old and new, at home and abroad. Long haunted by endemic indigence, India has lifted hundreds of millions out of extreme poverty since 1990; but even now one in five Indians is poor, the country is plagued by massive – indeed growing – inequality, and low-income states are home to almost half the population. With ten to twelve million new job seekers a year over the next decade, the government faces a huge challenge in terms of job creation, education, and training. New Delhi will also need to ensure a healthy and sustainable future for the people, and the socioeconomic inclusion of rural India in a country where, despite rapid urbanisation, 60% of the population are expected to still be living in rural areas in 2030.

As India's rise on the world stage progresses, the country also has to face a whole new set of regional and international challenges. In addition to the ever-present tension with neighbouring Pakistan and the international terrorist threat, China's growing assertiveness in the region poses a new and increasingly complex problem for India. This is especially true as Beijing steadily expands its influence in South Asia and the Indian Ocean, an area which India has traditionally considered part of its own sphere of influence. Competition with China may have prompted India to build partnerships with Japan, Australia, the USA and others; but New Delhi still struggles with the legacy of its longstanding policy of non-alignment, refuses to make fully-fledged alliances, and is uncertain what to do next in order to better its position in the regional balance of power.

As India and its citizens push ahead to a new place on the international stage, this ISPI Report is ultimately an effort to understand whether the world's largest democracy is ready to unlock its massive economic, political and human potential to realise its ambitions. Much of the answer to this riddle will depend on India's ability to tackle and overcome the multidimensional challenges it faces in an era of global disruption, rebalancing of power and multipolar competition.

What are the key political and economic reforms India needs today, if it is to pursue regional and global leadership? This question is at the core of Gautam Chikermane's opening chapter. After a review of the "first-generation" reforms that have shaped India's gradual opening to the world since 1991, the author provides an in-depth analysis of five key reforms which the government should deliver during the next 25 years, in the areas of land ownership, labour, infrastructure, agriculture and direct taxation. These second-generation reforms should not only be designed to consolidate the political and economic achievements of recent decades and to strengthen India's standing among its regional neighbours, but should also help the country move even faster in its quest to become a global superpower.

India's surge forward is taking place at a time when the world economy is being shaped by a new set of forces, including a slowdown in global trade and investment and the increasing impact of new technology on both manufacturing and services. How will its economy adapt to these changing conditions? While the world's largest democracy may in the past have fallen behind in the race to join global manufacturing value chains, Bidisha Ganguly argues in her chapter that India now has a new opportunity to take the lead in this transformed business world where goods and services are increasingly bundled together. Of course, there are still challenges – not least the need to accommodate a million new job-seekers every month, and to create productive jobs for a vast number of unskilled workers. In an environment of increased protectionism, however, India's large domestic market has an inherent advantage, one that the country's governments should build on to engage more fully with global trade and ensure that the country's products and services become more competitive.

The size and economic influence of the middle class have always been defining indicators of the soundness and health of any advanced industrialised economy. India should be no exception as it strives for regional power status: but does an Indian middle class actually exist? What are its features, and what role is it called upon to play in fulfilling the expectations of present-day India? These are some of the recurring questions that arise whenever there is talk of India's economic potential. There are great expectations – especially in the private sector – that the emergence of a large pool of increasingly affluent consumers will be the key development that turns India into the most vital market of the future. Moreover, there is hope that a solid middle class will generate the trickle-down effect needed to make India a less unequal society, not least by emancipating itself from caste rigidities in the medium term and by becoming part of a sound tax base. Are these expectations realistic? In the third chapter of this Report, Antonio Armellini analyses the characteristics, challenges and current trajectories of India's middle class, a demographic group that has long been the elusive holy grail for a country seeking recognition as an industrialised world power.

If hopes are high that the emergence of a solid middle class will finally reward India's impressive growth story, it is undeniable that the country is no stranger to inequality among its citizens, with disparities across its regions and states. Interestingly, an increasing number of studies show that the gap is further widening. India may have made momentous progress in reducing poverty, pulling hundreds of millions of people out of extreme indigence, yet, it seems that over the last three decades, the gains of growth have neither been matched by an increase in the equality of wealth and opportunities for all, nor by the convergence in the economic fortunes of richer and poorer Indian states. Nicola Missaglia's chapter argues that if both of these domestic challenges are not addressed swiftly, they pose the serious risk of translating into socio-political instability and centrifugal trends that could soon become a bottleneck on the path of India's rise to the world stage.

If a "superpower" is a state able to exert global or at least regional influence, a significant portion of such power-projection capacity – alongside economic, technological, commercial and diplomatic assets – consists of military strength. India is a nuclear power with huge armed forces, strategically located in the middle of the Indian Ocean. It is also one of the world's biggest arms importers, and continues to sign multi-billion-dollar arms deals with Russia, the USA and other competing vendors; the ultimate object of India's defence procurement is a matter of widespread speculation. Against this backdrop, in the fifth chapter Abhijit Iyer-Mitra assesses the multiple threats and security dilemmas India faces today. Its global ambitions notwithstanding, the author argues, the country still struggles to fully grasp its situation and work out the political steps it needs to take if it is to leave behind the strategic ambiguity that is becoming dysfunctional in a world shaped by the emergence of new military powers and shifting alliances.

The rise of China as a global economic, commercial, and even military superpower is causing considerable headaches for New Delhi, Beijing's main competitor in the region. The two countries have a long and ambivalent relationship that has often been described in terms of conflict and containment or, on the contrary, peaceful competition and cooperation. On the one hand there are many sources of bilateral tension, including un-resolved border issues, China's close relations with Pakistan, its growing naval presence in the Indian Ocean and its increasing economic influence in the region through the Belt and Road Initiative – a project India has refused to endorse. All these have prompted New Delhi to intensify multilateral cooperation with others likewise interested in containing China's assertiveness: Japan, the USA and Australia. On the other hand, China is India's biggest trading partner; both countries belong to the BRICS grouping and the Shanghai Cooperation Organisation, and they have established new forms of cooperation in recent years. Even India's relationship with the BRI is a complex one, for New Delhi knows that if it continues to shun the project it could nevertheless be gradually drawn into the net of relation-ships involving its neighbours. To explain the multiple layers of this complicated relationship in a rapidly changing world, Christian Wagner's chapter points out some of the national, regional, and global dilemmas and challenges which China pos-es for India, and explores its new strategies and initiatives in response to the BRI.

As the centre of economic and geopolitical gravity steadi-ly shifts towards Asia – not least because of the demographic and economic growth of China and India – Europe finds it-self obliged to engage more closely with the region, and a part-nership with India would give it a tremendous opportunity to build a long-lasting and mutually beneficial relationship with a "like-minded" country. But does Europe still offer India a means of nurturing its global ambitions? What should Europe's "grand strategy" concerning India look like today? And what role should Italy – one of India's top five trading partners with-in the European Union – play in this context? These are the main questions in Claudio Maffioletti's concluding chapter of this Report, which surveys the challenges and opportuni-ties implied by India's rise, both for Europe and for individual European countries – for our own in particular.

For decades India engaged only with reluctance in international politics. Eager to protect its democracy and its development from the bipolar competition of the Cold War, the country clung to non-alignment and self-sufficiency, disinclined to engage with the outside world. Since then, however, boosted by economic liberalisation and by the effects of rocketing growth, its aspirations have begun to transcend its immediate surroundings. At first they were regional; but today they are global, and Indians are confident that their country deserves a greater role on the world stage. A remarkable book published in 2010 asked whether India was now "ready to fly", but concluded that it was not: the country's phenomenal growth had not yet freed the "caged phoenix". Ten years later, the growing reality of a multi-polar world might offer India the right opportunity to assert its role as a leading player on the global scene. Whether the time has indeed come for it to become a fully-fledged great power – a "system maker" – is precisely what this Report is about.

Paolo Magri
ISPI Executive Vice President and Director

1. India's Turn: Groundbreaking Reforms for a Global India

Gautam Chikermane

In the evolving sphere of public policy, there are five big reforms India needs today – land, labour, infrastructure, agriculture and direct taxes. These are reforms that citizens have been demanding for decades, the intellectual base and arguments for which are in place, and political discussions have begun. They lie atop the reforms that are already in place since 1991, when the economy began to open up, and comprise second-generation reforms. Driving them is the fact that, although the political expressions and priorities may differ, the reforms process has not stopped. In fact, if we examine India's policymaking process, it is one of continuity.

From the creation of regulators to oversee various sectors – securities markets in 1992[1], telecom in 1997[2], competition in 2002[3], for instance – to the introduction of the Goods and Services Tax (GST) in 2017, arguably the most complex economic law in India[4] – irrespective of the nature of power

---

[1] "The Securities and Exchange Board of India Act", Ministry of Law and Justice, Government of India, 4 April 1992.

[2] "The Telecom Regulatory Authority of India Act", Telecom Regulatory Authority of India, 28 March 1997.

[3] "The Competition Act, 2002", Competition Commission of India, 13 January 2003.

[4] The law envisages one Constitutional Amendment [The Constitution (One Hundred and First Amendment) Act, 2016, Constitution of India]; four Central Acts of Parliament [The Central Goods and Services Tax Act, 2017;

structures, reformist policies have been crafted across a dynamic and changing political spectrum. Regardless of the government in power or the texture of the coalition that supported it, economic growth as a currency of political consolidation that began in the mid- to late-1980s and got a political boost in 1991, has strengthened and continues to date. In fact, economic growth that was seen to be an irritant in the state's wealth distribution priority in the first four decades after India's independence in 1947, has today become a political compulsion, a starting point upon which rests the governance edifice of jobs, entitlements and aspirations. This chapter examines the past 25 years of economic reforms and pushes for their continuity over the next 25 years. After this, or perhaps earlier, would be difficult to forecast, given the fast-paced developments in technologies, particularly artificial intelligence, robotics, and biosciences.

The process of economic reforms that decisively began under the "unlikely trio"[5] of Prime Minister Pamulaparti Venkata Narasimha Rao, Finance Minister Manmohan Singh and Principal Secretary Amar Nath Verma in 1991, with five pathbreaking and direction-inducing initiatives through the Statement on Industrial Policy[6], has continued across governments. What started under Prime Minister Rajiv Gandhi as arguably the most impactful highway-building initiatives through the National Highways Authority of India Act[7] has expanded since then through the "km per day"[8] race across successive

---

The Integrated Goods and Services Tax Act, 2017; The Union Territory Goods and Services Tax Act, 2017; and The Goods and Services Tax (Compensation to States) Act, 2017]; 29 State laws; and one Central notification for the seven Union Territories.

[5] R. Mohan, *The Road to the 1991 Industrial Policy Reforms and Beyond: A personalized Narrative from the Trenches, India Transformed: 25 Years of Economic Reforms*, New York, Penguin Random House, 2017.

[6] G. Chikermane, *70 Policies that Shaped India*, Observer Research Foundation, 2018, pp. 81-82.

[7] Ibid., pp. 79-80.

[8] "Shri Nitin Gadkari sets Award and Construction targets for the Road Ministry: Over 16000 km of NH to be constructed and 25 per cent higher more NH

coalitions to build more roads, right down to Prime Minister Narendra Modi. So too in the social sector – the Pradhan Mantri Jan-Dhan Yojana[9] in 2014 or the Pradhan Mantri Jan Arogya Yojana[10] of 2018, launched by Modi, are extensions and evolutions of the financial inclusion policies and the Rashtriya Swasthya Bima Yojana[11] scheme launched by his predecessor, Prime Minister Manmohan Singh.

The 1991 reforms under Prime Minister Narasimha Rao – arguably the most intense, with the greatest pressures on the economy, politically the most difficult, and with the highest delivery in terms of creating economic growth and poverty reduction – today may be seen as first-generation reforms that opened the economy to markets, private and foreign capital, and outsourced their governance to regulatory institutions. They gave relatively greater freedom to entrepreneurs on the licencing side but continued to keep controls on the inspection side – the infamous Licence Raj was reduced, but the brutal Inspector Raj continues. The command-and-control regime has diminished, but not ended.

The first-generation reforms followed a balance of payments crisis at the beginning of the 1990s. It was successfully averted following a 17.3% devaluation against the pound, the sale of gold – 20 tonnes to Union Bank of Switzerland for US$200 million and 47 tonnes to the Bank of England for US$405 million – and a US$1.2 billion IMF programme between 1991 and 1993[12]. As part of the IMF package, India initiated

---

[9] Pradhan Mantri Jan-Dhan Yojana, Department of Financial Services, Ministry of Finance, Government of India.

[10] PM launches Ayushman Bharat – PMJAY at Ranchi, Prime Minister's Office, Government of India, 23 September 2018.

[11] Rashtriya Swasthya Bima Yojana (RSBY) – Highlights, Press Information Bureau, Ministry of Labour and Employment, Government of India, 24 March 2013.

[12] A. Ghosh, "Understanding Pathways Through Financial Crises and the Impact of the IMF", *India, Global Governance*, vol. 12, no. 4, October/December 2006,

works to be awarded this year", Press Information Bureau, Ministry of Road Transport & Highways, Government of India, 17 April 2018.

economic reforms. Although the reforms have been far-reaching and extensive, the overarching philosophy of state control and serving an entitled government service continues – the inability to privatise the national airline, Air India, is a stark example of this abject failure. The manner in which sectors have opened up also remains confounding. Within financial services, for instance, 100% FDI is allowed in mutual funds, 74% in private banks, and 49% in insurance and pensions. How any one of these sectors is more crucial than the other remains a mystery. Or take infrastructure: while oil and gas exploration and production comes with 100% FDI, it is restricted to 49% in petroleum refining[13].

The post-2019 reforms need, among other things, to smoothen and standardise these limits. While the 1991 reforms came with one foot off the fiscal cliff, the benefits of which have trickled down in the form of reduced poverty and a strong economy, the political acceptance of reforms as a tool for prosperity is at best ambiguous[14]. For instance, agriculture – the sector whose contribution to GDP has been systematically falling and yet is supports the livelihoods of half the population – remains in the economic backwaters. So, the specific policy shift that looks at doubling farmers' incomes from simply providing food security is the political economy answer for those left behind. Similar tensions exist in reforming the two most important areas of labour and land.

---

pp. 413-429.

[13] "Consolidated FDI Policy", Department of Industrial Policy and Promotion, Ministry of Commerce and Industry, Government of India, 28 August 2017.

[14] For a larger discussion see: A. Kumar, "Dissonance between Economic Reforms and Democracy", *Economic and Political Weekly*, vol. 43, no. 1, 5-11 January 2008, pp. 54-60; K.C. Suri, "Democracy, Economic Reforms and Election Results in India", *Economic and Political Weekly*, vol. 39, no. 51, 18-24 December 2004, pp. 5404-5411; S. Kumar, "Impact of Economic Reforms on Indian Electorate", *Economic and Political Weekly*, vol. 39, no. 16, 17-23 April 2004, pp. 1621-1630.

The First 25 Years of Reforms

The story of India's economic reforms is as much a story of macro challenges, democratic expression, political evolution, bureaucratic grid-locking and institutional change on the domestic side as it is of strategic relocation, technological hyper-jumps, ideological shape-shifting and pressures of "great power" expectations in the field of international affairs. To look at India's reforms in isolation, decoupled from politics, foreign policy and information-age disruptions, would be examining the crust without delving deeper into the innards. In the world's largest democracy, beneath economic indicators such as gross domestic product (GDP) and competitiveness or fiscal deficit and human development indices, lie several constraints and compulsions. It is not enough to open markets and sit back and watch the genie of freedom deliver prosperity – each percentage point of growth needs attentive nursing. The biggest danger is incumbent beneficiaries leaning on simmering socialist and communist ideologies to whip up political passions against reforms. This battle will be hard fought. The road towards a middle-income economy to which India aspires is built by the collective will of the people that finds expression in freedoms, institutions, the law, and the dust of democratic wrestling matches, all captured within the confines of the constitution through buttons on electronic voting machines.

Within the confines of economics, India stands out as a nation of contexts and contrasts. In terms of size, at US$2.6 trillion, India's GDP is the world's sixth largest, after the US, China, Japan, Germany and the UK[15]. On a projected GDP growth of 7.3% in 2018 and 7.6% in 2019[16] – making it the fastest-growing large economy, ahead of China's 6.6% and 6.3% respectively, but close to smaller economies such as Bangladesh, Bhutan and Myanmar – India would have climbed

[15] World Bank Open Data, accessed on 30 October 2018.
[16] *Asian Development Outlook 2018 Update: Maintaining Stability Amid Heightened Uncertainty*, Asian Development Bank, September 2018.

one notch higher to fifth rank by end-2018, crossing the UK on the way. The way India is reorganising doing business is also on an upward trajectory. In Doing Business 2018, India's ranking rose 30 points to 100[17], a big leap by any standard; in Doing Business 2019, India's rank improved further to 77[18] and remains among the "top 10 improvers". In terms of being competitive, India ranks 58[19], down 19 points from the previous year's rankings[20] – above South Africa (rank: 67) and Brazil (72) but below China (28), Italy (31) and Russia (43).

But with a per capita income of US$1,940, India lags behind the world – it is less than a fifth of the world average, a quarter of China's, one-sixteenth of Italy's, and one-thirtieth of the US[21]. Since each dollar goes farther in India due to purchasing power parity (PPP), India's per capita income based on PPP stands at US$7,056[22]; ranked 125, it lags behind El Salvador, Bolivia, and Timor-Leste, and is less than half of China's and the world average, and one-fifth of Italy's, South Korea's and Israel's[23]. In terms of human development indices, India has reached the ranks of "medium" human development but ranked at 130 after Guatemala, Tajikistan, and Namibia, and the path to global averages is not far – a life expectancy at birth of 68.8 (world average: 72.2) or expected years in school at 12.3 (12.7), for instance. To arrive where China is today, India needs to climb 44 rungs[24].

---

[17] *Doing Business 2018: Reforming to Create Jobs*, A World Bank Group Flagship Report, World Bank Publications, 2018.

[18] *Doing Business 2019: Training for Reform*, A World Bank Group Flagship Report, World Bank Publications, 2019.

[19] K. Schwab, The Global Competitiveness Report 2018, World Economic Forum, 2018.

[20] K Schwab, The Global Competitiveness Report 2016-2017, World Economic Forum, 2016.

[21] World Bank Open Data (2018).

[22] Ibid.

[23] Ibid.

[24] Human Development Indices and Indicators: 2018 Statistical Update, United Nations Development Programme, 2018.

When looked at through the prism of international relations, the story of India meanders through frictions created by strategic choices and ideological fault lines. On attaining independence, India's principles of foreign policy stood on three legs – cooperation with the United Nations, nonalignment, and "upholding of weak and oppressed nations"[25]. Ideologically, in the initial years of its Independence in 1947, India embraced socialism. This was possibly a rebellion against its colonial past and probably a demonstration of freedom. In the ensuing Cold War between the US and the Soviet Union, the former saw India's path of nonalignment as a "morally bankrupt position" and urged India to get on the "democratic side immediately"[26], while the latter attempted to pull the most important nonaligned nation towards itself, with its MIG fighters finally tilting the scales towards Five-Year plans[27] and the Indo-Soviet Treaty of 1971 sealing it[28].

Finally, there has been a shift in India's democratic propulsions. Although coalition politics began tentatively in the states of Bihar, Uttar Pradesh, Punjab, Haryana and Madhya Pradesh in 1967[29], it was not until the formation of the Janata Party government in 1977 (a catalyst of structural change[30] even though the party could not endure) that it reached the centre. Both

[25] A. Appadorai, "India's Foreign Policy", *International Affairs*, Royal Institute of International Affairs, vol. 25, no. 1, January 1949, pp. 37-46.

[26] R.J. McMahon, *The Cold War on the Periphery: The United States, India, and Pakistan*, New York, Columbia University Press, 1994, p. 40.

[27] D. Rothermund, "India and the Soviet Union", *The Annals of the American Academy of Political and Social Science*, vol. 386, November 1969, pp. 78-88, Sage Publications.

[28] M.R. Masani, "Is India a Soviet Ally?", *Asian Affairs: An American Review*, vol. 1, no. 3, January/February 1974, pp. 121-135.

[29] See P.R. Brass, "Coalition Politics in North India", *The American Political Science Review*, vol. 62, no. 4, December 1968, pp. 1174-1191; A. Ratna, "Impact of Coalition Politics on Constitutional Development of India", *The Indian Journal of Political Science*, vol. 68, no. 2, April/June 2007, pp. 337-354.

[30] J. Das Gupta, "The Janata Phase: Reorganization and Redirection in Indian Politics", *Asian Survey*, University of California Press, vol. 19, no. 4, April 1979, pp. 390-403.

imploded under the weight of their internal contradictions. As a result, the first four decades after Independence were largely dominated by a single party, the Congress, both at the centre as well as in the states. Riding a relatively deregulated and definitely more open economy, the last three decades have seen a surge of political parties, again at the centre as well as in the states, each giving democratic expression to slivers of constituents, across regions, religions and castes. While the coalition era began to crystallise from 1991 onwards, as economic growth delivered political spaces, the past two governments – two terms of the Congress-dominated United Progressive Alliance (UPA) and one of the BJP-led National Democratic Alliance (NDA) – seem for the moment to have established cross-party politics as the fulcrum of India's political direction, replacing the rainbow of coalitions in the Congress years that thrived by co-opting diverse constituencies.

The economic monster that policies built over the first four decades of India's independence created – command-and-control economy, government to manage the "commanding heights", state-driven growth, excessive licences, disproportionate inspectors, and an overall sense of looking at wealth creators as criminals, a practice whose remnants remain alive even today – began to eat into the vitals of the nation. It was only when policymakers realised they were teetering on the edge of a balance of payments crisis that change began to come.

Beginning on 24 July 1991, the Indian economy took a major shift in stance by means of a string of policies that included abolishing licences for most industries, allowing greater flexibility in FDI approvals, de-reserving sectors the public sector could function in[31]. Powered by pre-reform policies, India's GDP growth rose from an annual average rate of 3.5% between 1951 and 1979 to 5.6% between 1980 and 1990. After crashing to 1.4% in 1991 following a balance of payments crisis that ignited economic reforms, growth took off – it was 6.5%

---

[31] G. Chikermane, *70 Policies that Shaped India…*, cit.

between 1992 and 1996, 5.4% between 1997 and 2002, and 7.8% between 2003 and 2015[32].

At a projected growth rate of between 7% and 8%, India is today the world's fastest-growing large economy. It has been able to shed its ambiguous past and is moving towards a decisive growth trajectory – within the mixed economy confines. It may be pertinent to point out, however, that India has always been a leading economy in terms of size[33]. It was ranked among the top 10 economies between 1960 and 1973; between 1974 and 1990, it ranked between 9 and 13; with one exception in 2010, between 1991 and 2014 – the time when the economy was undertaking major reforms – its rankings ironically fell to between 10 and 19. The dramatic return to the top 10 followed. India ranked 7 in 2015 and 2017, and 6 in 2017. Given the convergence of forecasts of growth rates – 7.3% by the World Bank[34], International Monetary Fund[35], and Asian Development Bank[36] – India ranked 5 by end-2018.

The Next 25 Years of Reforms

If the last 25 years have brought India to a point where its markets are being sought after, its entrepreneurs relatively freed, its consumers more empowered, and its politics a little closer to economics, the next 25 years of reforms need to first consolidate these, remove the disharmonious wrinkles in policy and then craft new reforms that will help India accelerate at a faster pace. Among the new, India needs to look at five specific reforms. These reforms will drive India's economic and political journey over the next quarter century. They will pave the path

---

[32] M. Singh Ahluwalia, "India's 1991", in R. Mohan (ed.), *Reforms, India Transformed: 25 Years of Economic Reforms*, Penguin Random House India, 2017, p. 56.

[33] World Bank Open Data (2018).

[34] World Bank, *Global Economic Prospects, The Turning of the Tide?*, June 2018.

[35] *World Economic Outlook. Challenges to Steady Growth*, International Monetary Fund, October 2018.

[36] Asian Development Bank (2018).

on which India could grow almost six-fold to a US$15 trillion economy. Inequality notwithstanding, they will be the markers of a US$10,000 per capita income that would leave poverty in the records of history. They will set the tone for India's expression as a regional if not a global "great power", tackling the two hegemonies of the US and China on more equal terms than it can today. They will bring a military heft, not merely on land but more importantly in the Indian Ocean region. They will strengthen India's strategic partnerships with the US and the EU, and give it the power to stand up to China's regional hegemony.

Two-and-a-half decades from today, the India of 2044 would definitely be a more capitalist entity. The economic aspects of this transformation would be underlined by a knowledge society, based on information, its related technologies and the work-life ecosystem surrounding it. But it would also be one that would be politically underlined by welfare economics. It would continue to be driven by entitlements. The reforms undertaken today would deliver growth in both GDP as well as in the tax-GDP ratio. Given the current trends in tax collection and the backend digital infrastructure that can capture every transaction digitally, leakages would be minimised and a tax-GDP ratio of 30% would be within reach. The resultant US$4.5 trillion worth of state financial capacity, about 1.8 times India's current GDP, would finance a never-before-seen infrastructure build-up, supported by social sector schemes, and a stronger footprint towards funding a deeper and wider role in international affairs.

Land Reforms

The foundation of all infrastructure creation and manufacturing is a four-letter word: land. And for reasons that have their basis in the annals of history, in the memories of people whose properties have been snatched, and in the poorly conceived and shabbily executed compensation and resettlement policies of the Indian state since Independence, land has become an emotive and political issue. The credibility of laws, lawmakers and executing bodies, be they private or public, concerning land acquisition has become so low that people can be easily organised around it and thrown into the melting pot of violence. Between 1947 and 2004 about 25 million hectares of land (more than the area of the United Kingdom) had been acquired for various purposes – building dams or special economic zones, for instance. This displaced 60 million people[37] (about the population of Italy), a third of whom[38] have yet to see any resettlement. As a result, the inherent suspicion of and aversion to giving up land for "national causes" is backed by a cultural and inter-generational memory of exploitation. Better to hold on to land at any cost rather than to trust the state, goes the underlying thought.

On the other side stand arguments for infrastructure-driven and manufacturing-led economic growth. Through these will come the accompanying societal benefits such as jobs, well-being, and prosperity. These will deliver the taxes that will fund domestic social sector schemes and entitlements, expand India's foreign policy endeavours, and facilitate a deeper and more meaningful engagement with issues such as climate change and millennium development goals. Here, land becomes the key constraint. The struggle of the people on the ground was reflected in parliamentary debates and resulted in enactment of the Right to Fair Compensation and Transparency in Land Acquisition, Rehabilitation and Resettlement Act, 2013[39], which attempted to fix some of the anomalies. Under this law, private firms need to acquire 80% of land through negotiations, with the government stepping in only for the remaining

---

[37] *Development Challenges in Extremist Affected Areas*, Report of an Expert Group to Planning Commission, Government of India, April 2008.

[38] K. Murali, M.A. Vikram, "Land Acquisition Policies - A Global Perspective", *International Journal of Scientific and Research Publications*, vol. 6, no. 5, May 2016.

[39] "The Right to Fair Compensation and Transparency in Land Acquisition, Rehabilitation and Resettlement Act", Legislative Department, Ministry of Law and Justice, Government of India, 26 September 2013.

20%; for government, infrastructure or PPP projects, the limit is 70%. These limits are difficult to implement. On the commercial side, the cost of land needed for infrastructure projects has risen four-and-a-half times[40], making any business case out of tune with ground reality.

As seen from above, within the confines of India's borders the policy's execution is bad enough; look outside and the contrasts become stark. The definition of public purpose, for instance, is wide and includes strategic and national security needs on the one hand and the regular requirements of the government or of the private sector on the other[41]. A 31 December 2014 Ordinance[42] attempted to narrow this and exclude projects vital to India's security and defence, but it has lapsed. In Malaysia, the government can acquire land for "public purpose", which includes residential, agricultural, commercial, industrial or recreational purposes[43]. Australia defines public purpose as one in which parliament has power to make laws, making the process open ended[44]. A small nation like Singapore faces different challenges and has tailored policies to include the state acquiring land for residential, commercial or industrial purposes[45]. Talking about land acquisition in China is futile, as the authoritarian regime has little patience for democratic rights. But when

[40] D.K. Dash, "Govt payout to acquire land for NHs rises 4.5 times in 4 years", *The Times of India*, 14 December 2018

[41] "The Right to Fair Compensation and Transparency in Land Acquisition, Rehabilitation and Resettlement Act", Section 2, Legislative Department, Ministry of Law and Justice, Government of India, 26 September 2013.

[42] "The Right to Fair Compensation and Transparency in Land Acquisition, Rehabilitation and Resettlement (Amendment) Ordinance", Legislative Department, Ministry of Law and Justice, Government of India, 2014.

[43] "Land Acquisition Act", Section 3(1)(c), The Commissioner of Law Revision, Department of Director General of Lands and Mines, Ministry of Natural Resources and Environment, Government of Malaysia, 1960.

[44] *Lands Acquisition Act 1969*, Section 6, Definitions, Federal Register of Legislation, Office of Parliamentary Counsel, Australian Government.

[45] "Land Acquisition Act", Section 5(1)(c), (Chapter 152), The Statutes of the Republic of Singapore, The Law Revision Commission, Legislation Division, Attorney-General's Chambers, Government of Singapore.

Indian businesses compete with those from other nations, land becomes a key constraint – and one that the new government will need to fix.

Labour Reforms

The other big elephant in the room is labour laws. While nobody is arguing for the absolute supremacy of capital as a factor of production over labour, the fact that India has 37 central laws[46] and six amendments relating to various aspects of labour

---

[46] "The Employees' Compensation Act", 1923; "The Trade Unions Act", 1926; "The Payment of Wages Act", 1936; "The Industrial Employment (Standing Orders) Act", 1946; "The Industrial Disputes Act", 1947; "The Minimum Wages Act", 1948; "The Employees' State Insurance Act", 1948; "The Factories Act", 1948; "The Plantation Labour Act", 1951; "The Mines Act", 1952; "The Employees' Provident Funds and Miscellaneous Provisions Act", 1952; "The Working Journalists and Other Newspapers Employees (Conditions of Service) and Miscellaneous Provisions Act", 1955; "The Working Journalists (Fixation of rates of Wages) Act", 1958; "The Employment Exchange (Compulsory Notification of Vacancies) Act", 1959; "The Motor Transport Workers Act", 1961; "The Maternity Benefit Act, 1961; The Payment of Bonus Act", 1965; "The Beedi and Cigar Workers (Conditions of Employment) Act", 1966; "The Contract Labour (Regulation and Abolition) Act", 1970; "The Payment of Gratuity Act", 1972; "The Limestone and Dolomite Mines Labour Welfare Fund Act", 1972; "The Bonded Labour System (Abolition) Act", 1976; "The Iron Ore Mines, Manganese Ore Mines and Chrome Ore Mines Labour Welfare (Cess) Act", 1976; "The Iron Ore Mines, Manganese Ore Mines and Chrome Ore Mines Labor Welfare Fund Act", 1976; "The Beedi Workers Welfare Cess Act", 1976; "The Beedi Workers Welfare Fund Act", 1976; "The Sales Promotion Employees (Conditions of Service) Act", 1976; "The Equal Remuneration Act", 1976; "The Inter-State Migrant Workmen (Regulation of Employment and Conditions of Service) Act", 1979; "The Cine Workers and Cinema Theatre Workers (Regulation of Employment) Act", 1981; "The Cine Workers Welfare Fund Act", 1981; "The Dock Workers (Safety, Health and Welfare) Act", 1986; "The Child and Adolescent Labour (Prohibition and Regulation) Act", 1986; "The Labour Laws (Exemption from Furnishing Returns and Maintaining Registers by Certain Establishments) Act", 1988; "The Building and Other Constructions Workers' (Regulation of Employment and Conditions of Service) Act", 1996; "The Building and Other Construction Workers Welfare Cess Act", 1996; "The Unorganized Workers' Social Security Act", 2008.

shows how intense the legislative assault on capital has been and still is. For instance, there are six laws that are related to wages alone. Worse, there are separate laws for disparate sectors – beedi and cigar workers, newspaper employees, working journalists, limestone and dolomite welfare, labour welfare for iron ore mines, manganese ore mines and chrome ore mines, cinema workers and cinema theatre workers, dock workers, and building and other construction workers. This shows two things. First, either our lawmakers don't know how to draft laws based on firm principles and second, perhaps, there is an element of political grandstanding and entitlement disbursement to serve slivers of workers, giving the impression that a particular constituency is being helped rather than the entire labour force. We need a deeper study of these laws and to compress them into two – one for physical aspects such as safety, the other for financial aspects such as wages and social security.

Such is the scale and complexity of laws that the Inspector Raj combined with litigation has become par for the course. A simple concept of wages, for instance, has as many as eleven definitions in the corpus of Indian labour legislation. Each piece of labour legislation that needs to be enforced requires the maintenance of a separate register and submission of annual returns to the authority designated in the act and its rules, which not only costs valuable time and money but also adversely affects the implementation of labour standards, besides ironically making the cost of compliance higher than the cost of violation[47]. With 429 different types of scheduled employments where the minimum wage rates have been fixed by the centre or the states[48], resulting in more than 1,200 minimum wages coexisting in India[49], the one certain outcome it has de-

---

[47] A.N. Sharma, "Flexibility, Employment and Labour Market Reforms in India", *Economic and Political Weekly*, vol. 41, no. 21, 27 May to 2 June 2006, pp. 2078-2085.
[48] *Report on the Working of the Minimum Wages Act, 1948 for the Year 2014*, Labour Bureau, Ministry of Labour and Employment, Government of India, 21 August 2016.
[49] B. Varkkey, R. Korde, *Minimum Wage Comparison: Asian Countries: Official*

livered is the strengthening of the Inspector Raj – just one state (Tamil Nadu) carried out 126,856 minimum wage inspections in 2014 alone[50]. Clearly, a rational businessman would prefer to violate labour laws at the lesser cost of bribing the inspector or paying the measly fine imposed by the courts[51].

The fact that India has a rich culture of entrepreneurship is despite laws, not because of them. These laws could have served a public-political purpose in the past. But the XXI century entrepreneur has XXI century options. Between artificial intelligence and robotics, for instance, the need for labour is diminishing, first in the high-tech industries but slowly into others such as carmakers. Between 3D printing and the Internet of Things, the requirement of hands is being replaced by the need for skills; these technologies as well as those who can run them are trickling down, both in terms of prices as well as access. Between a relatively more open economy today and the domestic constraints on entrepreneurs, it is not so difficult to invest on foreign shores. It is only a matter of time before India's archaic laws that seem to have been enacted for, and/or captured by, a hugely entitled and unionised workforce serving tiny pockets, keeping the huge mass of India's workers out of factory economics, turn obsolete and irrelevant. The political upshot of such a scenario – and it is not too far in the future – will be devastating for a labour-surplus economy like India.

The choices before India's policymakers aren't many. The key is to arrive at a balance that protects the welfare of labour without hurting the interests of capital, all the while functioning under the invisible force of market mechanisms. It is necessary to realise that the labour-management relationship is not a zero sum game but a synergistic association, a mutualism, where one feeds and carries the other towards growth, and where both serve a bigger and more organised capital source. This source is the

---

Representation of Minimum Wages, Indian Institute of Management Ahmedabad, June 2012.

[50] *Report On The Working Of The Minimum Wages Act, 1948 For The Year 2014…*, cit.

[51] A.N. Sharma (2006).

savings of citizens, of which labour itself is a part, that go into provident funds, mutual funds, insurance and pension funds, which in turn invest them in the companies that entrepreneurs create. This is the virtuous cycle of capitalism. Its ills, such as excessive greed or fear, cannot be regulated by any government entity or laws. There is only one regulator here – the market.

The problem is not in redrafting laws, rules and regulations; most ideas are already on the intellectual table. The challenge is to effectively communicate these ideas to the entitled, while reaching out to those who are excluded from organised labour. One way out would be for policymakers to focus on income security (through social security schemes in case of a lay-off) rather than job security (guaranteeing people the same job till retirement) for workers. Above all, India needs to end the Inspector Raj that allows the lower bureaucracy to extract revenues and replace it with self-assessment and self-certification, backed by technology-driven pipelines that transparently capture, measure and influence worker-management behaviour. Essentially, to start looking at the entrepreneur as a partner, not a criminal.

Infrastructure Reforms

Neither land nor labour reform can reach fruition without the strength of infrastructure. It is only when roads are, or plan to be, laid that land becomes attractive, setting up industrial belts feasible, and hiring labour possible. But because of its constantly changing textures, not merely through varying sector-specific policies but across an overarching philosophy underlying it, India's infrastructure story often reads like a badly written novel, with several authors across multiple ideologies scripting a patchy, chaotic path with no climax in sight. Sifting through them brings three trends to life.

First, the shift to a public-private participation (PPP) model from one where the government and the public sector had the sole monopoly over the key sectors of the Indian economy. The Bhakra Nangal dam, for instance, was built entirely by means of public resources. It was conceptualised in 1944, approved in 1945, preliminary works began in 1946, construction in 1948, and the first phase completed in 1963[52]. On the other hand, the Indira Gandhi International Airport was built by GMR, a private enterprise, through a January 2006 agreement[53] to operate, manage and develop the airport for 30 years that can be extended by another 30 years. Both are large projects, both have huge capital and technological requirements, both need a high level of management post-completion of projects. But the former was built entirely by the state, the latter by the private sector.

Second, the swing from complete control to partial control through the creation of regulatory bodies. From a point where the hand of the government loomed over any large infrastructure project and micromanaged it to the last nail to one where the compliance function has been outsourced to a relatively independent regulatory body to draft rules and ensure delivery, this is a big leap. The regulator could oversee extraction of natural resources oil and gas[54], the creation of highways[55], ports[56] or telecommunications[57], for instance. Such a structure also brings transparency and disclosures into the sector, and enforces the rule of law under the supervision of appellate bodies.

---

[52] Developmental History of Bhakra – Nangal Dam Project, Bhakra Beas Management Board.

[53] *Delhi Airport. Operation, Management and Development Agreement between Airports Authority of India and Delhi International Airport Private Limited for*, Ministry of Civil Aviation, Government of India, 4 April 2006.

[54] Directorate General of Hydrocarbons, Resolution No. 0-20013/2/92-ONG D III, Ministry of Petroleum and Natural Gas, Government of India, 8 April 1993.

[55] "The National Highways Authority of India Act", Section 3A(1), Ministry of Law and Justice, Government of India, 16 December 1988.

[56] "The Land Ports Authority of India Act", Legislative Department, Ministry of Law and Justice, Government of India, *The Gazette of India*, 31 August 2010.

[57] "The Telecom Regulatory Authority of India", India Code, Legislative Department, Ministry of Law and Justice, Government of India, India Code, 28 March 1997.

And third, the move to private sector or mixed financing models from one where the government or public sector financed these projects. Here, the government needs to ensure that while it is outsourcing financial requirements to the private entrepreneur, there must be enough on the table after delivering public objectives for the entrepreneur to offer her investors. Profit, a word that has gathered ugly textures as the Indian economy charted the socialist path from Independence till 1991 – fragments of which are visible even today – is a necessary condition for banks, insurance and pension funds to invest money for such long-term projects.

Two things are clear. One, the government does not have the resources to build a XXI century infrastructure for India. And two, the market in the form of the private sector is willing to invest. What is needed is to rethink infrastructure policymaking that takes these two vectors into account. This means designing policies that leave room for a changing dynamic of financing patterns or technological disruptions, for instance, and allowing contractual renegotiations where necessary. In a world that is besieged by new and often project-changing information that businesses need to work with and adapt to, the rules and regulations appended to those projects also need to move with the times. Shifting infrastructure building to a principles-based approach rather than a rules-based straitjacket may help ease the pressure. This shift need not be absolute – a principles-based architecture that focusses on outcomes supported by rules-based regulations could be an ideal mix to capture the best of both, stability and flexibility.

Communicating with stakeholders across the spectrum through policy disclosures and transparency (putting every rule and regulation up for public debate before enforcing it, for instance) would go a long way in building consensus. Further, capacity-building needs expertise, and expertise requires knowledgeable people. Rather than making regulatory bodies sinecures for retired bureaucrats[58], merit and expertise must override all other considerations. The governance architecture for regulators put together by the Financial Services Legislative Reforms Commission[59] is a good model that can be expanded across non-financial regulators as well. Bringing in apolitical professionals from engineering, law, big data, finance and accounts into the regulatory ambit, as executives or consultants, would help sharpen regulatory drafting. Further, every rule must have a reason for existence, a logic that supports that reason, and which rests on the foundations of a cost-benefit analysis (benefits must outweigh costs). Regulation of infrastructure is really an outsourcing of the government's law-making powers and regulators, while being given independence on the functional side, must remain accountable on the governance side; crafting that balance is a new skill that needs working on, as the recent fiasco between the Reserve Bank of India and the government has shown[60].

While these are broad directions, there is no single silver bullet to fix infrastructure – telecommunications require a level of oversight different from oil and gas, airports and urban development have unique regulatory needs, the complexities of power and water supply are not the same, the financing needs of roads and ports stand on economics separate from those of railways. If India is able to reboot its stance and relook at infrastructure as a lever to reach a US$10 trillion GDP and a middle income economy through long-gestation projects that thrive across governments of different hues, only then would India's infrastructure story reach a fitting finale. The trinity that

---

[58] P.S. Mehta (ed.), *Regulatory Authorities: selection, tenure and removal*, Centre for Competition, Investment and Economic Regulation, 2007, p. 192.

[59] *Analysis and Recommendations*, volume I, *Report of the Financial Sector Legislative Reforms Commission*, Ministry of Finance, Government of India, March 2013, pp. 21-27.

[60] G. Chikermane, *RBI versus the Government: Independence and Accountability in a Democracy*, Occasional Paper no. 179, Observer Research Foundation, December 2018.

has delivered speed to India's economic system with its actions so far now needs to deliver stability, and through it infuse credibility into the political system.

Agricultural Reforms

The fact that in 2019 the focus of India's agricultural policy has shifted to delivering higher returns to farmers from simply creating food security for the nation speaks volumes about the progress the sector has made over the past seven decades. Today, the policy focus is on doubling farmer's incomes by 2022 through an increase in productivity of crops, crop intensity, production of livestock, and price realisation on the one side and a reduction of the costs of inputs through higher efficiency, diversification towards high-value crops, and shifting cultivators to non-farm jobs on the other. This the government proposes to do by unpegging fruits and vegetables from the minimum support price mechanism, along with institutional reforms such as introducing private mandis (agriculture marketplaces), increasing contract farming, and enabling direct farmer-to-consumer sales[61]. All these ideas are worth pursuing.

Concurrently, and within the confines of constitutional segregation of powers between the centre and the states, a legislative process to fix anomalies has begun. In order to make efficient use of cultivable land – currently constrained by restrictive tenancy state laws, landowners and cultivators are forced to resort to informal agreements that leave both insecure – an expert committee has proposed a new law, the Model Agricultural Land Leasing Act, 2016[62]. The law, under which leasing agricultural land is being made more flexible, including standard agreements, grants protection to both parties and could reduce the legal hurdles obstructing farm efficiency through better

---

[61] R. Chand, *Doubling Farmers' Income: Rationale, Strategy, Prospects and Action Plan*, NITI Policy Paper no. 1/2017, National Institution for Transforming India, Government of India, March 2017.

[62] *Report of the Expert Committee on Land Leasing*, NITI Aayog, Government of India, 31 March 2016, pp. 18-37.

utilisation of land. After it goes through the process of deliberation, such a reform would enable better use of agricultural land. In terms of crop productivity, taking just two main crops, India ranks low. In wheat, India's 3.20 metric tonnes per hectare (mtph) is below China's 5.48 mtph, Mexico's 5.24 mtph, or the world average of 3.47 mtph. In rice, India's 3.87 mtph is less than US's 8.41 mtpa, South Korea's 7.01 mtph, Japan's 6.78 mtph or the world average of 4.54 mtph[63]. Apart from enabling productivity reforms here, the sector also needs physical investments so that farmers can shift to more value-added crops. But in order to start cultivating fruits and vegetables, farmers would need storage facilities. Already, losses across crops range from 3.4% to 5% for pulses, 2.2% to 9.1% for oilseeds, and go as high as 4.2% to 13.9% for fruits and 4.6% to 11.0% for vegetables[64]. Specifically, losses stood at 15.9% for guavas, 12.4% for tomatoes (18.2% at retail level), 7.9% for sugarcane, 7.2% for eggs and 10.5% for seafood. The estimated annual value of these losses stood at Rs 927 billion[65].

Various governments have been attempting to fix this but have not been able to. Now, with parliamentary sanctions[66] behind this idea, taking them forward has the will of the people and reforms here should become relatively easier. What may not be so easy would be dismantling the minimum support pricing mechanism, now more a political tool serving vested

[63] United States Department of Agriculture, Foreign Agricultural Service, Circular Series WAP, 12-18 December 2018.

[64] S.K. Nanda, R. Vishwakarma, H.V.L. Bathla, A. Rai, and P. Chandra, *Harvest and post harvest losses of major crops and livestock produce in India*, All India Coordinated Research Project on Post Harvest Technology, Indian Council of Agricultural Research, September 2012.

[65] S.N. Jha *et al.*, *Report on Assessment of Quantitative Harvest and Post-Harvest Losses of Major Crops and Commodities in India*, ICAR-All India Coordinated Research Project on Post-Harvest Technology, ICAR-CIPHET, 27 March 2015.

[66] Implementation of Scheme for Integrated Cold Chain and Value Addition Infrastructure, Standing Committee on Agriculture (2016-2017), Sixteenth Lok Sabha, Ministry of Food Processing Industries, Forty-Fifth Report, Lok Sabha Secretariat, August 2017.

interests than an economic one[67], and nudging farmers towards market-led diversification, thereby ending the dictum that India may be a "foodgrains secure" country but not necessarily "food secure"[68].

Returns from such market-friendly policies would impact not merely the farmers – they would contribute to the growth of the sector and through it the economy, create jobs and opportunities in rural areas, utilise and drive infrastructure creation, and help India move towards greater crop productivity. It would also reduce the pressure to move to the cities for employment or livelihoods. Above all, it would change the texture of politics in rural India and help transition the 60% of Indians who live in the countryside to better living standards.

Direct-Tax Reforms

Both the leading national political parties of India, the Bhartiya Janata Party (BJP) and the Indian National Congress (INC) share one thing in common: both have felt the need for, and followed it up with, legislative proposals for direct-tax reforms. And not without reason. In a country where just 46.7 million individuals and 1.1 million firms paid income tax in 2017-2018[69], leaving a huge chunk outside the tax network, this needs a policy rethink and legislative intervention. The current tax infrastructure comprising laws, rules, regulations and the army of officials executing it needs a reorganisation. Between the complexity of tax laws on the one side and a revenue-seeking tax bureaucracy on the other, the case to stay out of the tax network and evade taxes is strong. With successive governments trying to widen the tax base, what is heartening is that a clean-up has begun on both sides.

---

[67] G. Chikermane, *70 Policies that Shaped India…*, cit. p. 38.
[68] *Report of the Expert Committee to Examine Methodological Issues in Fixing MSP*, Ministry of Agriculture, Government of India, 27 June 2005, p. 32.
[69] Income Tax Return Statistics Assessment Year 2017-2018, Version 1.0, Income Tax Department, Government of India, October 2018.

The direct tax to GDP ratio that stood at 2.2% between 1950 and 1960 and at 5.7% between 2008 and 2015[70], was close to 6% during 2017-18, the highest in the last 10 years[71]. With India's total tax to GDP ratio at 16.8%, the country has a long way to go – the average tax-GDP ratios of Organisation for Economic Cooperation and Development (OECD) nations stood at 34.2% in 2017 – more than 40% for seven countries including Italy, France and Denmark, and above 20% for the US, South Korea and Lithuania. The only country among OECD nations to match India's numbers is Mexico with a tax-GDP ratio of 16.2%. But change is in the air. The number of total returns filed has jumped to 68.5 million from 37.9 million over the last four years, an increase of more than 80%, while the number of individuals filing returns has risen by 65% to 54.4 million from 33.1 million[72].

Introduced in July 2017, the well-conceptualised but badly executed Goods and Services Tax (GST) should deliver on the indirect taxes front, but there remains a vacuum on the direct taxes side. The incumbent BJP-led government, as the previous Congress-led coalition earlier, have been trying to fix this through the enactment of a new law, the Direct Taxes Code. While the earlier dispensation had made two attempts to approve the law, one each in 2009[73] and 2013[74], the incumbent government has formed a task force to draft new legislation[75]. A bill that proposes to consolidate and amend the laws

---

[70] M. Govinda Rao, S. Kumar, *Envisioning Tax Policy for Accelerated Development in India*, NIPFP Working Paper Series, no. 190, National Institute of Public Finance and Policy, 28 February 2017.

[71] CBDT releases Direct Tax Statistics, Press Information Bureau, Ministry of Finance, Government of India, 22 October 2018.

[72] Ibid.

[73] The Direct Taxes Code, 2009, National Portal of India, National Informatics Centre, Ministry of Electronics & Information Technology, Government of India, 12 August 2009.

[74] The Direct Taxes Code, 2013, Income Tax Department, Ministry of Finance, Government of India, 1 April 2014.

[75] Constitution of Task Force for drafting a New Direct Tax Legislation, Press

dealing with direct taxes – the Income Tax Act, 1961, and the Wealth Tax Act, 1957 – into a single and simple law, this is a much-needed policy intervention that has five goals. First, to make taxation more predictable than it is. Second, to reduce the cost of compliance and administration. Third, to minimise exemptions that serve a particular constituency and create a base for their expansion. Fourth, to reduce the ambiguity that facilitates tax avoidance. And fifth, to stem tax evasion. Sitting on these five legs, the goal is to increase the tax-GDP ratio.

Noble and desirable as the objectives are, if the legislative complexity and executive bureaucratise of the GST is a lesson in how to destroy a good law by burdening people with excessive compliance, these crucial direct-tax reforms are best left alone till a time when the executive and bureaucratic focus leaves the overarching on-ground administrative approach that focusses on revenue-extraction and replaces it with one that catalyses and serves them. It needs deep debate. It needs political will that is, unlike in the case of GST, backed and supported by bureaucratic transformation. Without it, we will end up having a well-intentioned law that would be little more than the status quo.

Conclusion

These five reforms may appear to be too specific in their outlook, too narrow in their sectors and too limited in their outcomes. They need three bigger institutional reforms – administrative, political and judicial – as catalysts. But, as argued, their impact will overflow and trickle down into not merely into other areas but also impact the economy through an increase in economic growth and a decrease in inequality. Being low-hanging policy fruits, they will deliver efficiency into the system, across three large policy and economic trajectories of agriculture, manufacturing and infrastructure. In turn, these will impact services

Information Bureau, Ministry of Finance, Government of India, 22 November 2017.

that sit astride this trinity, and deliver the two most important political outcomes – low inflation and high job creation. But the challenges are many too. Entrenched interests around labour and land would create frictions. Business interests may collide among themselves as well as institutions to keep harvesting the status quo. Political alignments will turn them into virtue signalling ideas with which to capture constituencies. All of whom are legitimate actors in the dance of the world's largest democracy. How it negotiates these challenges will define India's place in tomorrow's world.

2. How Solid Is India's Economy?

Bidisha Ganguly

Rapid growth over the last decade and a half has placed India among the ten largest economies in the world and it is not inconceivable that it will be among the top three in another decade or so. Herein lies India's key strength: being counted among the major country groupings such as the G20 and BRICS. Its demographic profile as a country with a large number of young people has attracted attention. At a time when most countries are grappling with the problems of an ageing population, India has the asset of a large working-age population and a lower dependency ratio.

Of course, the youth bulge comes with its own set of problems – with many of them not able to find productive jobs, they are often a destructive force rather than the driver of growth that conventional economic literature expects them to be. In other words, there is no automatic translation from having a young population to experiencing higher growth. The government faces the tough challenge of educating the workforce and creating appropriate jobs. While the share of agriculture in GDP has been declining, the manufacturing and services sectors have not been able to adequately absorb the workforce employed on the farms.

After the liberalisation measures taken in 1991, India has had a market economy, which successive governments have tried to encourage and support. Economic reforms implemented to foster a more open and market-based economy include opening the market to domestic and foreign private investment across many sectors that were earlier protected, a business-friendly

taxation and regulatory regime and deepening of financial markets. Perhaps the biggest change is apparent in the relaxation of
restrictions in the foreign exchange market. India's currency is
now widely traded with many of the restrictions on current and
capital account transactions now lifted.

Features of the Indian Economy

A large economy

India not only ranks among the ten largest economies in the
world but is also one of just three members from developing
economies in that list (Figure 2.1). As a result, India often represents key concerns of emerging economies in areas ranging
from trade to climate change to financial stability. Country
groupings such as the G20 or BRICS (a group of emerging
economies) have been formed to articulate the policy views of
a more representative group of economies. For example, India's
commitment and efforts to step up the use of clean energy has
been noted as commendable by bodies such as the UN.

FIG. 2.1 - NOMINAL GDP ($ BN) OF TOP 10 COUNTRIES, 2018

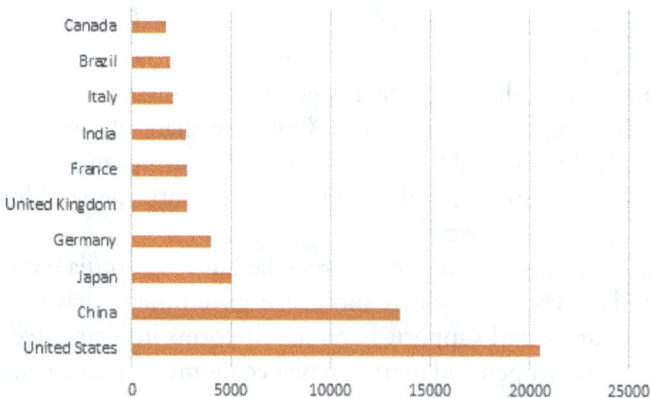

Source: International Monetary Fund

India, with the lowest per capita income among these economies, is also considered a land of opportunities that is bound to
catch up with its richer counterparts in the emerging economic
universe. As the country grows and its people move up the income ladder, the demand for a range of products will keep increasing. At a time when many markets have reached a level of
saturation and demand is often scarce, this is indeed welcome.
Businesses are keen to tap the potential of an economy with
high domestic demand.

India's ratio of private consumption to GDP is high at 58%
while its investment ratio is also significant at 30%. This trans-
lates to a sizeable demand for not only consumer products
ranging from staples to durables but also for infrastructure and
construction related products. For example, India has emerged
as the fourth largest market for automobiles. As a result, all major automobile makers have invested in India and this has led
to a globally competitive supply chain of vendors in the auto
component sector.

Growing consistently at 6-7%

India has seen consistent growth for the last two to three decades since the economic liberalisation of the 1990s. Real GDP
growth increased from 6% during the first ten years (1991-
2001) to 7.7% during the next (2001-2011) and 6.9% during the current decade so far (2011-2017). The consistency of
this performance has reinforced confidence among investors
that changing governments have not resulted in any significant
change in the economic performance of the nation. The chart
below shows India's growth performance since 2005-2006 and
it is apparent that even after the sharp dip in growth in 2008-
2009 (due to the global financial crisis), the country was able to
recover and grow consistently in the following decade.

FIG. 2.2 - REAL GDP GROWTH 2005-2006 TO 2017-2018

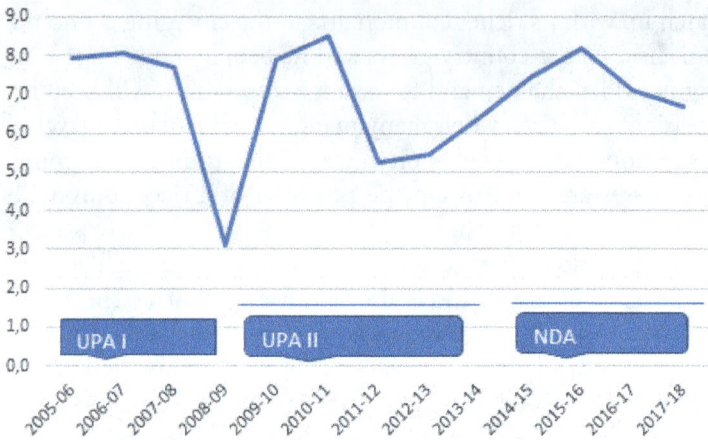

Source: Central Statistics Office

Dominated by services

Historically, developing economies have moved from being predominantly agrarian to being dominated by industry. A dominant services sector has typically emerged at a later stage when an economy is more advanced. India has defied this pattern to emerge as a significant player in services while its manufacturing sector has remained a relative underperformer.

This pattern of development is in contrast to both textbook theories and the actual experience of many Asian economies that have been able to step up the average income levels of the people by generating mass employment at factories. India, on the other hand, has relatively few mass manufacturing enterprises with labour-intensive production. Economists have most often blamed inflexible labour laws and various regulatory bottlenecks for India's lack of success in labour-intensive, export-oriented industries.

FIG. 2.3 - SHARE OF SECTORS IN GDP (%)

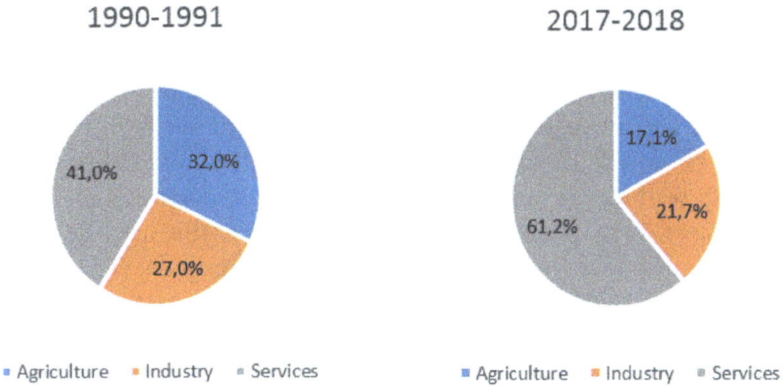

1990-1991

2017-2018

Source: Central Statistics Office

This has been termed "premature de-industrialisation" by some authors, indicating a failure to ignite a critical stage of development.

Instead, India's GDP is dominated by the services sector, which by nature tends to be inward looking. Of course, India has had tremendous success in developing an export-oriented IT services sector. However, the bulk of services such as domestic transportation, logistics and retail, real estate and construction are non-tradable. Many purists insist that only manufacturing can deliver the vast number of low-skill jobs that India needs while others say that services are equally capable, especially in an era when most businesses are expected to provide a mix of manufacturing and services to attract customers.

Growing openness in trade and investment

Since the early 1990s, the trend has been towards a more open economy that is deeply integrated with the global economy. The ratio of trade to GDP has doubled from around 15% in 1990-1991 to 30% as of 2017-2018. In addition, several regulatory changes have led to much greater inflows and outflows of capital, which was earlier restricted. Increasing financial integration is indicated by much higher foreign direct and portfolio investments (FDI and FPI) into India. For example, gross FDI into India touched US$60 billion in 2016-2017 and 2017-2018, with India rivalling China as the top destination for FDI.

However, the openness has also revealed a critical weakness of the Indian economy – the fact that it imports much more than it exports on a consistent basis. While this need not be regarded as a weakness, it does make the country dependent on foreign capital inflows to fill the deficit. These inflows include not only FDI but also very volatile portfolio investments in the debt and equity markets. When these inflows are high, the currency tends to appreciate while it depreciates when there are outflows. These movements tend to be self-reinforcing, leaving the monetary authority with very little control over the exchange rate.

Fig. 2.4 - Foreign portfolio investment and exchange rate (average)

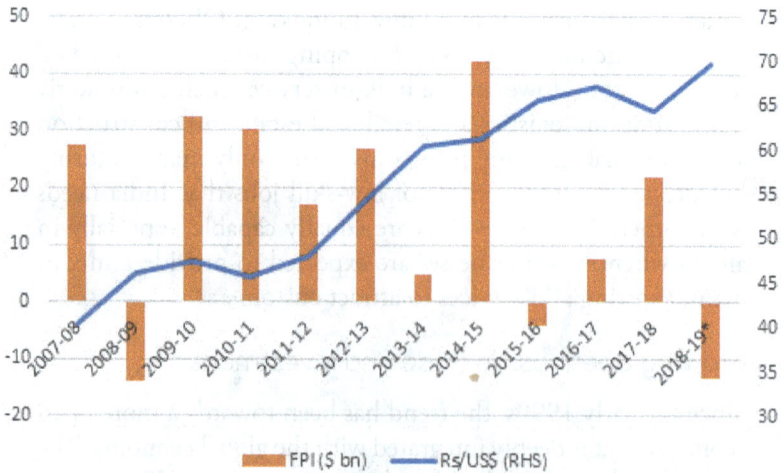

Source: Reserve Bank of India; *Apr-Dec

In 2018, for example, the rupee depreciated sharply over the year, as the prospect of rising interest rates in developed countries, particularly the US, led to an outflow of capital from India. The impact was exacerbated due to the concurrent rise in oil prices which led to a widening of the current account deficit (CAD). The CAD, which amounted to 1.9% of GDP in 2017-2018, rose to about 2.7% in the first half of 2018-2019. Volatility in oil prices and capital inflows will continue to have an impact on the exchange rate. At the same time, when compared to other emerging market currencies, the rupee was able to recuperate much of its losses by the end of 2018 so that its loss was contained to about 9% against the US dollar during 2018. In contrast, the fall in the Argentine peso and the Turkish lira were much sharper, at 102% and 39% respectively. India's higher growth rate and continuing reforms makes it a less risky place to invest in.

World's largest democracy

Perhaps India is best known for being the world's largest democracy and this aspect has implications for the economy as well. Many have commented that India's economic policies cannot be as bold as China's, where the government can take tough measures without fear of being voted out. This is most apparent in areas such as infrastructure creation or labour reforms where India has often stumbled. Land can be an emotive issue and state governments have been toppled on issues of land acquisition without adequate compensation. Similarly, labour laws provide excessive protection to the currently employed at the cost of larger numbers of people finding employment.

India's economic policies have had a history of socialism, which came under attack in the 1990s as free market capitalism emerged across the world as the dominant ideology. Many of the economic reforms implemented during that decade, such as reductions in import tariffs and in direct tax rates, did not find much resistance from the electorate. Indeed, it led to the emergence of the middle class, which was expected to form the support base for more reforms. However, India's middle class remains small relative to its population and is usually outweighed by the greater weight of the poor as a political force.

That said, there is now a strong constituency for development, as evidenced in the national election campaigns of 2014 and 2019. Every government, including at the local and state level, strives to demonstrate its good performance in improving the quality of peoples' lives through better provision of amenities such as power, physical connectivity and housing. Subsidies and handouts have become less important, though not non-existent. A recent lamentable development has been the proliferation of farm loan waivers by state governments as a response to incidents of rural distress. This has had negative fallout on the general credit culture.

Strong business community

India has had the advantage of a strong business community established since the nineteenth century. Entrepreneurial energy has been an active force that has survived the restrictions of the socialist era and has been rejuvenated after economic liberalisation in the 1990s. As in much of Asia, businesses are dominated by the family-run and it is only recently that companies with large organisations and a clear separation of ownership and management have emerged. The success of Indian companies in creating wealth is evident from the significant rise in market capitalisation on the stock exchanges. At the end of 2017, the total value of listed companies was US$2.3 trillion, an increase of 1.4 times from its value in 2010.

Yet the business community has also come under attack recently for not being transparent. Political discourse has increasingly targeted rival political parties for being close to so-called "big business". The reality is that while some businesses may have committed fraud, many have also suffered due to unexpected hurdles. In the infrastructure sector, for example, projects have not been completed as they have come up against bottlenecks in acquiring land or getting government clearances.

To stay away from the political limelight, the business community needs to repair its image as a progressive force in the popular imagination. The government would then find it easier to partner with businesses in development and modernisation work.

The problems being faced by industry are reflected in the pile up of unpaid loans over the past few years. The gross non-performing assets (GNPAs) of the banking system touched a peak of 11.5% of outstanding credit in March 2018. After the government brought in new legislation on bankruptcy in 2016 to enable faster resolution of stressed assets, there has been some progress in resolution. However, as depicted in Figure 2.5, the ratio of GNPAs to GDP moderated for the first time in several years in September 2018. This has allowed bank lending to pick up quite substantially.

FIG. 2.5 - BANK CREDIT GROWTH AND NPAS

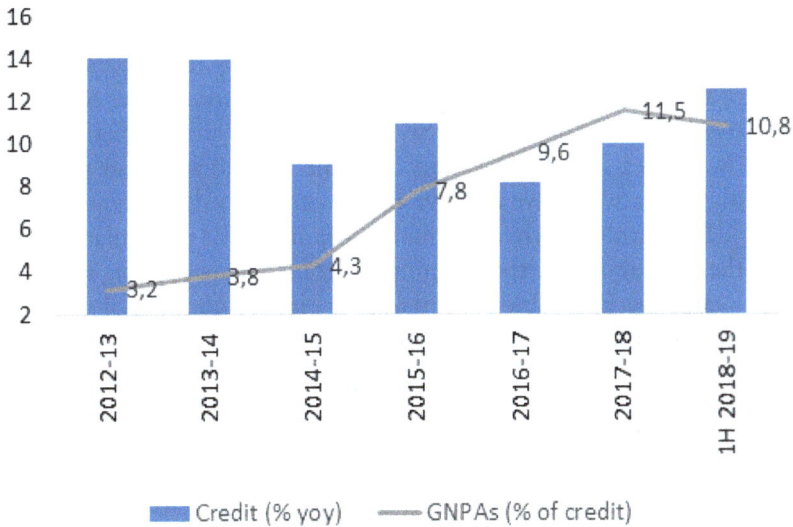

Source: Reserve Bank of India

Vision for the Future

The NITI Aayog (the think tank established by the Modi government in place of the erstwhile Planning Commission) recently brought out a document called Strategy for New India@75[1]. This envisages the building of a "development state" and sets clear goals for such a transformation to be achieved by 2022-2023 when India will celebrate 75 years since its independence in 1947. The goals are set out under four comprehensive sections – drivers, infrastructure, inclusion and governance. In this article, the focus will be on a few of them which I believe are critical to achieve.

Human development

India's performance on human development indicators has much room for improvement. The Human Development Index (HDI) constructed by United Nations Development Programme (UNDP) assesses progress on three basic dimensions of health, education and standards of living. India's rank on the HDI remains low at 130 out of 189 countries although the HDI itself has improved over the years. India is currently in the category of medium human development, along with most other South Asian nations other than Sri Lanka (high) and Afghanistan (low). Health and education outcomes in India remain poor, making it imperative to move ahead with focused interventions.

In education, while enrolment has increased particularly at the primary level, the learning outcomes remain poor. Poor-quality teaching, absenteeism among teachers and lack of monitoring of learning outcomes plague the public school system. Quality is even more of a challenge in higher education, with very few Indian institutions featuring in global rankings. The poor quality of higher education is also evident in the fact that affluent sections of society are increasingly seeking higher education abroad, with Indians now spending about US$6-7 billion annually on foreign universities.

---

[1] *Strategy for New India@75*, NITI Aayog, November 2018.

TAB. 2.1 - INDIA'S HDI RELATIVE TO OTHER COUNTRIES
AND GROUPS (2017)

	Life expectancy at birth	Expected years of schooling	Mean years of schooling	GNI per capita (2011 PPP $)	HDI Value	HDI Rank
India	68.8	12.3	6.4	6,353	0.640	130
Bangladesh	72.8	11.4	5.8	3,677	0.608	136
Pakistan	66.6	8.6	5.2	5,311	0.562	150
Sri Lanka	75.5	13.9	10.9	11,326	0.770	76
South Asia	69.3	11.9	6.4	6,473	0.638	-
Medium HDI	69.1	12.0	6.7	6,849	0.645	-

Source: 2017 Human Development Report, UNDP

Reforming the education system is extremely important for the future competitiveness of the country and its people. Vocational education needs to be incorporated into the education system. In fact, there must be a life-long learning process for acquiring new skills as technology progresses steadily making old skills redundant. Similarly, the public health management system needs to be upgraded for better human development outcomes. Moreover, the healthcare sector is one of the fastest growing, with the ability to absorb workers with a range of skill levels from doctors to nurses to medical lab technicians. The government's recent attempt at moving towards universal health coverage is commendable but will require massive efforts to implement within a reasonable time frame.

Agriculture

Agriculture accounts for only 17% of GDP but more than half of India's workers are employed in farming. It is therefore not surprising that the income from farming is inadequate and the younger generations no longer want to continue in this work.

It is in this context that the government has set a target of doubling farmers' incomes by 2022-2023. In a series of papers, NITI Aayog member Dr. Ramesh Chand has outlined the ways in which this can be achieved[2]. The three main contributors are a physical increase in crop production, better price realisation by farmers and finally, a reduction in the number of cultivators. He has shown that farm incomes can be doubled over a period of seven years, with each of the three factors contributing a third of the total increase.

Increased production can be achieved by various means such as raising productivity through higher investment in irrigation, diversification into high value crops and livestock and greater use of technology. Better price realisation requires reforms in the marketing and distribution of agricultural products that would lead to less intermediation. To this end, the government has created the e-NAM or electronic National Agricultural Market, an online trading platform for agricultural commodities. In addition, private investment to modernise the value chain is being sought to ensure a better deal for farmers.

Despite these changes, it is evident that the prices of food products have been falling recently (Figure 2.6). This has led to pockets of rural distress, which were widely blamed for the defeat of the ruling party in three state elections held in November and December 2018. This decline in food prices has come about even in the face of a government policy mandating a minimum support price (MSP) of 1.5 times the cost of production for each crop. The MSP is the price at which the government is mandated to buy agricultural products from the farmer though this is hard to implement beyond the staples of rice and wheat.

---

[2] R. Chand, *Doubling Farmers' Income: Rationale, Strategy, Prospects and Action Plan*, NITI Policy Paper no. 1/2017, National Institution for Transforming India, Government of India, March 2017.

FIG. 2.6 - CPI INFLATION - FOOD

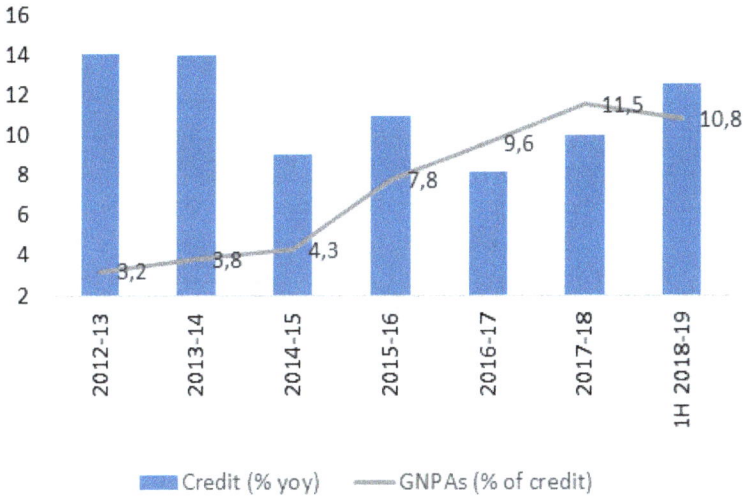

Source: Central Statistics Office

The third factor – a reduction in the number of people dependent on agriculture – is the most critical and would require economy-wide reforms to create jobs and livelihood opportunities. Broadly, there are two kinds of jobs that can be created – less skill intensive and highly skilled. While the policy regime needs to gear up for both, the surplus agricultural labour can probably be absorbed in relatively less skilled areas. What is needed is a flexible regulatory environment which allows businesses to scale up and hire with ease. Currently, regulations on labour as well as regulatory burdens on small and medium-sized enterprises act as a deterrent to increasing employment. This is why the vast majority of jobs (estimated to be above 80%) are in the informal sector where firms are not subject to regulations.

Infrastructure

Building better infrastructure has been a priority for every government, be it at the central or the state level. Some of the major projects that have been successfully completed in recent years include:

- Several major airports have been expanded and modernised by the private sector. Delhi airport is now among the 20 busiest airports in the world and is set for further expansion.
- The Airports Authority of India has developed and upgraded 23 metro airports in the last five years and plans to develop over 20 airports in non-metro cities.
- Between FY2014 to FY2018, over 32,000 km of highways were constructed. The six-lane Yamuna expressway connecting New Delhi to Agra was completed in 2012 and has dramatically reduced the travel time between the two cities.
- After starting operations in 2002, the Delhi metro has expanded continuously. At least 10 Indian cities are working on metro rail projects while the monorail has made a beginning in Mumbai.

However, in a country of 1.3 billion people, much more needs to be done in areas such as urban transportation, power and water supply and sewage treatment. There is also great demand for inter-state travel by bus and rail where safety concerns need to be addressed.

Lack of good quality infrastructure is a major concern for industry, as it hampers international competitiveness. Take, for example, power supply, which is not only unreliable but has costs exceeding those in competing countries. Most businesses need to invest in captive power supply, which must be limited in scale, thus increasing the cost per unit of power supply. The critical bottleneck in power supply is that state government owned power utilities do not have the financial resources to invest in upgrading their systems. They continue with a cross-subsidy regime charging high commercial tariffs while providing free power for agricultural use.

Improving physical connectivity and better logistics are essential for improving the competitiveness of the domestic industrial sector. Logistics costs in India remain high at around 14% of GDP, with multiple agencies involved in different modes of transportation. Movement of goods across states is another problem due to different documentation requirements. The government has envisaged the creation of multi-modal logistics parks as the way forward for reducing logistics costs and over 30 such parks have been approved for completion by 2022-2023. Several industrial corridors are also being built with multilateral funding in order to trigger industrial development and employment around specific locations.

Simultaneously, a massive programme for port-led industrialisation is being implemented to modernise ports, enhance port connectivity and stimulate port-linked industrialisation. Known as "Sagarmala", this ambitious programme entails a cost of around US$122 billion across 604 projects. Interestingly, as part of the project, 14 Coastal Economic Zones (CEZs) have been identified in the maritime states, creating synergy with the industrial corridors that are also on the cards. At the same time, the business environment around shipping and ports is being looked into so that turnaround time can be reduced to achieve global standards.

TAB. 2.2 - PROJECTS UNDER SAGARMALA

	No. of projects	Project cost ($ bn*)
Port modernisation	266	20.2
Port connectivity	213	34.8
Port-led industrialisation	57	66.0
Coastal community development	68	1.0
Total	604	122.0

Source: Sagarmala.gov.in; *converted from INR at Rs 72 per $

Financial market development

Given that massive resources are needed for India's development in the immediate future, the financial markets and banks must be able to ensure adequate availability of capital. India has fairly well-developed financial markets and also a strong banking system. One of the oldest exchanges in Asia, the Bombay Stock Exchange is among the top 10 major international exchanges with market capitalisation of over US$2 trillion. Indian corporations have been able to raise credit and equity worth US$500 billion from the financial markets in the last five years. Mutual funds' assets under management have been rising steadily, amounting to over US$300 billion at the end of December 2018. Yet, the potential for intermediation of funds through the domestic financial system is much more, considering that Indians save as much as 30% of GDP. Presently, however, households save more in physical assets such as housing rather than financial assets that can be intermediated, though the gap has been narrowing over the years (Figure 2.7).

FIG. 2.7 - HOUSEHOLD SAVINGS BY ASSETS (% OF TOTAL)

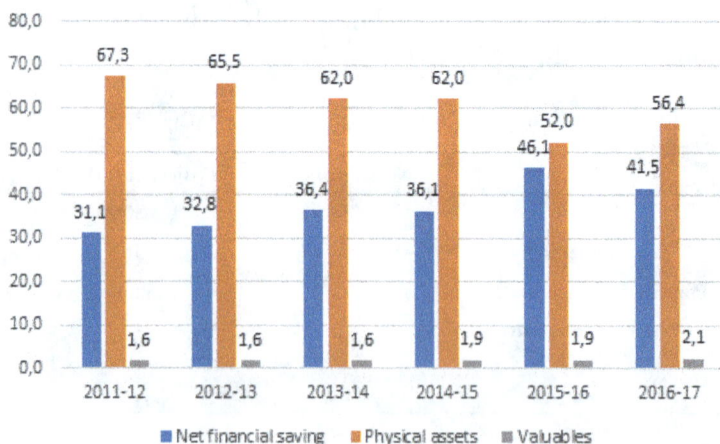

Source: Central Statistics Office

India has a mature commercial banking system with a deposit base of over 75% of GDP. Recent efforts at promoting financial inclusion have considerably increased the penetration of banking services, which is now 80%[3]. In terms of credit access, India is still lagging, with total credit to GDP ratio at 57% as of March 2018. The high cost of operating traditional branch-based banking and the lack of reliable financial information on small businesses are key impediments to increasing credit access, especially in rural areas and the informal sector. However, the ongoing digital transformation is bringing about change by enabling faster loan delivery. Cash flow data from Goods and Services Tax (GST) paying companies will enable banks to make a better assessment of their credit worthiness. As per estimates by Morgan Stanley[4], this could drive up loan growth to Micro Small and Medium Enterprises (MSMEs) to a high teen Compound annual growth rate (CAGR) over the next decade.

This trend of growing credit to smaller business and retail customers will also de-risk the banking system from over-dependence on large corporations for lending. With greater development of the bond markets, big companies will raise credit from the market rather than depend on bank loans. Episodes such as the recent build-up of non-performing assets (NPAs) in the banking system are also less likely when the ticket size of loans is smaller. The spread of mobile phone use, together with biometric identification (Aadhar) and GST, is expected to have significant impact on access to finance. The government is likely to benefit through improved tax compliance and higher tax collection.

[3] Global Findex database 2017, World Bank
[4] *India's Digital Leap – The MultiTrillion Dollar Opportunity*, Morgan Stanley Research, September 2017.

India and the World

GDP growth

How fast India is able to reach its development targets will depend not only on internal policy action but also on external developments in the global economy. Despite India's relatively more inward-looking economy, it will be hard to remain insulated from global trends in trade and investment. The global financial crisis in 2008, for example, was a setback for the global economy and India, too, experienced a slowdown in trade and investments flows, which led to a sharp slowdown in GDP growth to 3.1%.

The outlook for global economic growth is currently clouded with uncertainty, as risks to growth have escalated on account of trade tensions and tightening financial conditions. The IMF recently downgraded its growth outlook across both advanced economies and the developing world (Table 2.3). India is not only expected to be the fastest growing country at 7.5% in 2019 but is the only country for which 2019 growth is expected to be higher than in the previous year. Had the global outlook been rosier, India might have been able to grow at a faster rate.

Tab. 2.3 - World Economic Outlook: GDP growth (% y-o-y)

	2017	2018	2019 P	2020 P
World	3.8	3.7	3.5	3.6
Advanced economies	2.4	2.3	2.0	1.7
United States	2.2	2.9	2.5	1.8
Euro Area	2.4	1.8	1.6	1.7
Japan	1.9	0.9	1.1	0.5
Emerging and developing economies	4.7	4.6	4.5	4.9
China	6.9	6.6	6.2	6.2
India	6.7	7.3	7.5	7.7

Source: IMF

It may be pertinent to point out some lessons from China's growth path. China, which had stellar growth of over 10% for a long period of over 10 years, seems to be slowing down now. Chinese policymakers are trying to make the economy less dependent on debt-fuelled investment growth and more on consumption. China amassed a tremendous amount of debt during its high growth years, amounting to over 250% of GDP by mid-2018. Despite India's more conservative growth path (outstanding debt of around 125% of GDP), its banking system is already dealing with the NPA issue. It may therefore be prudent not to go for growth at all costs.

Trade

The outlook on global trade is also uncertain on account of emerging trade disputes between countries. Further, structural changes such as a decline in the trade intensity of global value chains is having an impact. It is apparent from Figure 2.8 that the performance of India's exports has been very significantly synchronised with global trade. The challenge for India will be to increase its share of global trade for which it will have to grow its exports at a faster rate than global exports for a few years. A comprehensive strategy focusing on exports should include ways to leverage the impact of the brewing global trade war, for example, by looking at newer products and markets. India's exports have traditionally found buyers in the developed Western markets but need to diversify to more lucrative developing nations where the penetration of Indian products such as textiles and pharmaceuticals is still low.

According to a McKinsey[5] analysis, the trade intensity of global value chains is declining while the flow of services and data now play a much bigger role in global trade. Labour arbitrage is becoming less important as a competitive advantage while knowledge intensity is rising. The coming decade is likely

---

[5] *Globalization in Transition: The Future of Trade and Value Chains*, McKinsey Global Institute, January 2019.

to be characterised by disruptions in technology and business models, and intense global competition and inter-connectedness. India is globally recognised as a leading player across a range of services but will now need to drive the new services paradigm of a digital economy. This encompasses both communication infrastructure and devices such as computers and mobile phones as well as technologies such as automation, artificial intelligence, data analytics, software platforms and cloud computing.

FIG. 2.8 - MERCHANDISE EXPORTS (% INCREASE Y-O-Y)

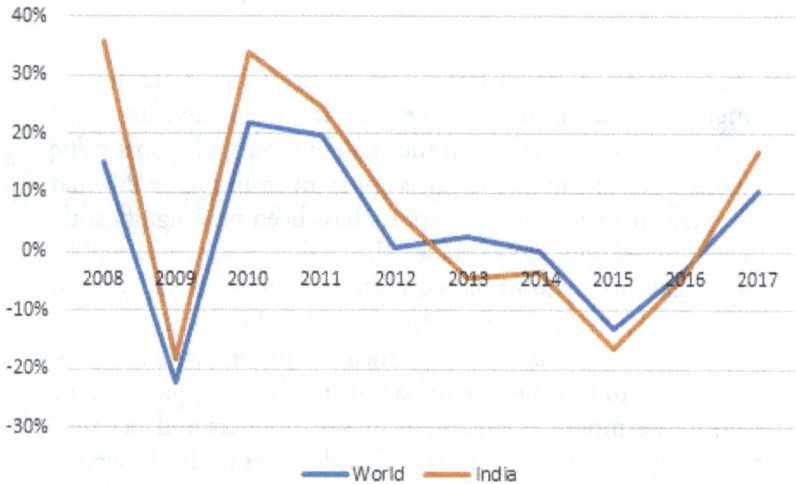

Source: World Trade Organization

Foreign Direct Investment

The global trends in FDI are not very comforting either: after falling by 23% in 2017, it fell again by 41% in the first half of 2018 (Figure 2.9). The reason, according to an UNCTAD study[6], lies mainly in the repatriation by United States parent companies of accumulated foreign earnings from their affiliates abroad following tax reforms in the US. The decline, however, was largely concentrated in developed countries while developing economies saw only a small decline. The uncertainty caused by tensions in global trade relations may also be making firms more cautious about investing in new locations. On a positive note, however, the decline in overall FDI is in contrast to a 42% increase in greenfield investments, which is an indicator of future trends.

FIG. 2.9 - GLOBAL FDI FLOWS (US$ BN)

Source: United Nations Conference on Trade and Development

As per India's balance of payments data, FDI inflows into India have steadily increased over the last few years but are likely to moderate slightly in the current year. The outlook is positive, given that the Indian government has made considerable

[6] Investment Trends Monitor, UNCTAD, October 2018.

efforts to attract foreign investment not only by relaxing controls across sectors but also by encouraging state governments to compete for investment. India is currently the tenth largest recipient of FDI and, with uncertainties looming in developed markets, more companies would look to the developing world for business opportunities. The improvement in India's ranking in the World Bank's Ease of Doing Business from 130 in 2016 to 77 in just two years has been noted as a sign of the government's intent to improve the regulatory environment. Transaction costs are being reduced in areas such as starting a business and trading across borders. The GST introduced in July 2017 has now stabilised and is allowing businesses to improve their operational efficiency.

Capital inflows

While FDI inflows are a stable source of capital, portfolio capital, which flows in and out of the country at a rapid pace, is more volatile. This poses a problem for India, as it needs capital to finance its current account deficit. The burst of reforms in the early 1990s included liberalisation of the capital account with measures such as allowing foreign institutional investors (FIIs) to invest in India's equity market. Since then, India attracts a fair share of global portfolio capital flows, having also partially opened up its debt market. In 2017-2018, for example, there were portfolio inflows of US$295 billion into India and outflows of US$273 billion, leaving a net investment of US$22 billion (Figure 2.10). With changing global financial conditions, the situation changed in 2018-2019 with net outflows of US$10 billion in the first half.

Such volatility in financial flows has a profound impact on the real economy through the exchange rate. In 2018, for example, the rupee had seen a rapid depreciation of around 15% by mid-October and the RBI's foreign exchange reserves had dropped by US$28 billion between April and December. The situation was just the reverse in the previous year when the RBI had to add US$54 billion to its foreign exchange reserves to prevent the currency from appreciating, as exporters complained that the currency was overvalued. When the correction came, it was too swift, leaving foreign investors and Indian holders of foreign debt with heavy losses. Financial conditions tightened as the RBI was not able to ease monetary policy despite falling inflation.

FIG. 2.10 - PORTFOLIO FLOWS (US$ BN)

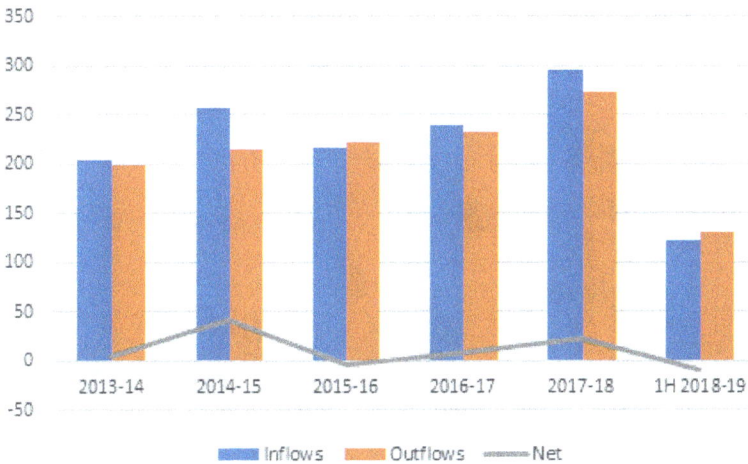

Source: RBI

The problem is that capital inflows and outflows into emerging economies such as India are largely driven by the monetary policy stance of the US Federal Reserve. So during the famous "taper tantrum" in May 2013 when the US Fed first announced its intention to normalise monetary policy from a position of extreme accommodation, there was a stampede of capital out of emerging economies and into the safety of the US Treasury. The RBI tries to smooth the volatility by buying dollars during periods of excess inflows and selling when there are outflows. But it cannot completely offset the movements in the currency that tend to have an impact on the ability of domestic businesses to compete with global players. Going forward, it seems likely that the US Fed will move to a more accommodative stance in view of softening global growth. This will enable the RBI to look forward to a period of relative calm.

FIG. 2.11 - FOREIGN EXCHANGE RESERVES (US$ BN)

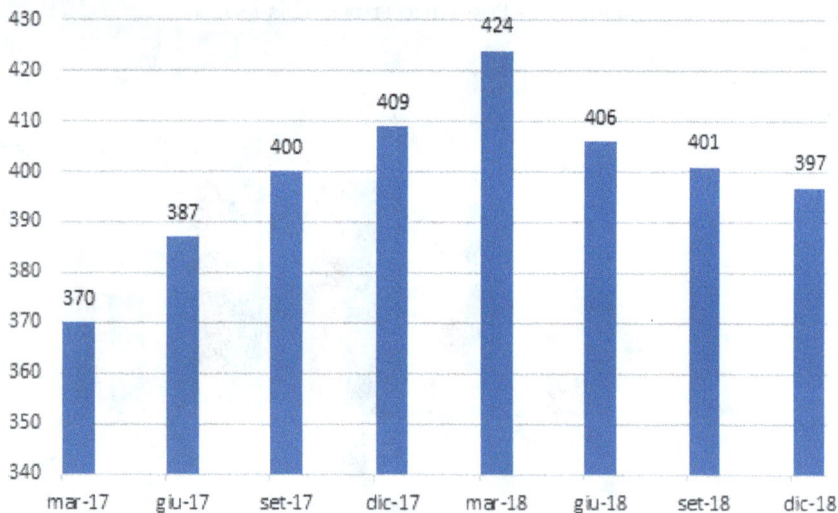

Source: Reserve Bank of India

Conclusion

India's development is taking place in an era where the global economic environment is being shaped by a new set of forces, what the Economist in a recent article has referred to as "slowbalisation". This is in contrast to the earlier era of globalisation in which a fall in the cost of transportation and telecommunication spurred a surge in global commerce and encouraged investments by firms with a global footprint. The trend in recent years is towards a slowdown in global trade and investments. Indian policy makers need to be aware of this so that they do not favour strategies that worked best in an earlier era. Businesses are also exploring the changes brought about by the fourth industrial revolution with technologies such as 3-D printing, machine learning and robotics.

These new technologies are gradually having a significant impact on the efficiency of the entire manufacturing process and the adoption of smart technologies is resulting in increasing automation for low-skill jobs, in both the services and manufacturing sectors. While India may have fallen behind in integrating into global manufacturing value chains, a new opportunity is now arising to be a leader in a transformed business world where there is increasing bundling of goods and services. Of course, this has led to much trepidation about how to create jobs for the vast number of unskilled workers who are currently underemployed. However, the pace of change in success factors will vary from sector to sector. For instance, labour costs and other current parameters for competitiveness may continue to be relevant, in the medium-term, for several sectors such as textiles.

As countries grow more stridently nationalist, globalisation is gradually giving way to increased protectionism and tightening trade regimes. Higher tariff and non-tariff barriers (such as standards, environmental issues, the labour-related, etc.) on select products are being introduced to protect the domestic industry. India with its large domestic market has an inherent advantage in an environment of increased protectionism. However, India needs to pursue greater global engagement in order to ensure greater competitiveness for its products and services. Moving ahead with regional trade agreements to get greater access to newer markets should be priority action for the government.

India's economy has displayed its strength time and again by not falling prey to various global and regional financial crises despite having a fairly globally integrated financial sector. External debt has remained moderate relative to other large economies. It has pursued the path of reform even when this has taken time and effort, such as to implement the goods and services tax or the insolvency and bankruptcy code. Both central and state governments have been able to achieve fiscal discipline even in difficult times. The Indian states are becoming increasingly aware of the need to create a business-friendly environment. For foreign investors seeking to invest in India, there are now many diverse opportunities presented by different states.

3. Defining the Indian Middle Class

Antonio Armellini

The Indian middle class has for long been the holy grail and elusive goal in the country's quest for recognition as an industrialised world power. To some extent, this can be ascribed to the difficulty of translating the inherently Western concept of middle class, with its attached history of social and industrial transformation, into a country that comes from a very different tradition and has not witnessed a real industrial revolution. The implications in terms of class structure of any such definition are problematic and could be a pointer to further contradictions; then there is the matter of caste and its relationship to class; again, an exclusively Indian conundrum. To conclude from this that the idea of middle class is on the one hand part of "left baggage" from the *Raj,* and on the other a purely economic and commercial indicator, would be tantamount to ignoring the role it is called to exercise – albeit in a different format – in the fulfilment of the expectations of present-day India.

Origins

The middle class in XIX century colonial India was essentially made up of persons directly or indirectly related to the *Raj* and its institutions. Its members were mostly high-caste Hindus or *ashraf* Muslims, were Western-educated, spoke English and had adopted customs and mores derived from their colonial masters; all characteristics that contributed to a sense of separation from the rest of the country's population. As an intermediate layer between the "decadent" nobility and zamindari classes, and the "plebeian" population at large, their role in respect of their colonial masters could be compared to that exercised in an equally socially immobile society – the XIX century Papal State in Rome – by the *Generone* class of doctors, lawyers, engineers and the like, versus the landowning papal aristocracy. Administrators both, the Indian middle class saw their role as purveyors of a modernity derived from the thinking of their progressive counterparts in Britain (which the *Raj* certainly did not share). Limited in numbers, their impact did not extend much beyond the élites of which they themselves were part but formed the basis for the development of a national consciousness, nurtured by those very same values.

In the attempt to address the contradictions between a Westernised ideological grounding and the quest for independent identity, the fathers of the national movement gave an increasingly prominent place to religion, as a means of spreading their message across a wider population. Such a move was designed to strengthen its political grounding but would have profound implications for the future, as noted by Sanjay Joshi: "electoral politics, combined with the search for 'authenticity'… led middle-class politics to transform a complementary religious nationalism into a competitive religious nationalism… (with) profound and long-term impacts on nationalist politics contributing in some measure to the horrors that accompanied partition"[1] and beyond.

The cultural hegemony of this Westernised middle class continued through the creation of independent India, where it was called upon at one time to ensure the continuity of the previous administrative structure, combining elements of modernity with those derived from tradition and religion. Not without peculiar points of contact between the two, such as in the

---

[1] S. Joshi, *India's Middle Class*, Oxford Research Encyclopedia, Asian History, Oxford University Press, April 2017.

perseverance of Victorian social strictures and prejudices, for example in matters of sexuality, well beyond their disappearance in the former mother country[2]. What the combination between the two would be in the new republican context was not a foregone conclusion – Jawaharlal Nehru was an out-and-out representative of the Anglicised élite but was aware of the danger of a disconnect between the middle class and the rest of the population; Mahatma Gandhi forcefully tried to remedy the imbalance by advocating a reversal of the roles of the two – and the debate was finally settled by a constitution that espoused the liberal principles of representative democracy, with some adjustments and unfinished business in order to leave space for other considerations – starting from language – that would have long-lasting and not always welcome implications in subsequent years. The dominance of Western-oriented élitist political culture continued through the subsequent years of socialist development, adapting to changing local conditions – patronage, corruption, regional contrasts etc. – and maintaining its fundamental imprint.

The cracks at the time of the Emergency, with Indira Gandhi's failed authoritarian attempt, and subsequent developments which led to the economic and financial crisis of 1991, signalled a change in the structure and priorities of government; the Nehruvian social model had to contend with market-oriented reforms based on the shift towards a capitalist-based economy. The political and cultural message of a mainly high-caste, Westernised and progressive middle class was being questioned by the emergence of new regional and local power centres, often populated by other castes, which gave way – in Sanjay Joshi's words - to a *rightward shift to a capitalist dreamworld dressed up in Hindu cultural nationalism*[3]. The "new middle class" combined all the above elements, had a broader social and caste

---

[2] In itself an interesting cause for reflection on the intricacies of the relationship between "Western" and "authentic" values in a country which has given the world the lesson of the joyous and liberated sexuality of Khajuraho.

[3] S. Joshi (2017).

basis and felt free from past cultural and ideological strictures in the pursuit of its own economic benefits. Its aspirational and self-centred character put in a different light the claim to represent an inclusive social and cultural reference point, leading Pavan Varma to denounce that "the policy of economic liberalisation provides the Indian middle class an excuse to even more blatantly separate its 'world' from the vast masses of the destitute and deprived"[4]. Religion acquired a greater role as the jelling agent of a middle class that sought to overcome its anxieties and contradictions through the creation of a distinctive separate Hindu identity in a globalised world but ended up providing space for intolerance[5].

Definition

Different methods have been tried to define the composition of India's "new middle class", as it is currently described. Identifying criteria go from income and wealth to educational levels, human development, behavioural measures and methods of self-assessment. None have acquired absolute value, but a generally recognised reference point is McKinsey's 2007 paper *The Bird of Gold*, based on a study by the National Council of Advanced Economic Research (NCAER)[6].

The McKinsey-NCAER study is income-based and divides the population into five groups: a) *deprived*, with yearly incomes below Rs. 90,000; b) *aspirers*, with incomes between Rs. 90,000 and 200,000; c) *seekers*, with incomes between Rs. 200,000 and 500,000; d) *strivers*, with incomes between 500,000 and 1 million; e) *globals*, with incomes exceeding 1 million, and it includes only the top three in the middle class.

[4] P.K. Varma, *The Great Indian Middle Class*, New Delhi, Viking, Penguin Books India, 1998.
[5] S. Khilnani, *The Idea of India*, New Delhi, Penguin, 2004.
[6] McKinsey Global Institute, *The Bird of Gold: The Rise of India's Consumer Market*, McKinsey&Co, May 2007.

There are many others:

- Homi Kharas places the emerging middle class at per capita daily income levels between US$10 (the poverty line in Italy and Portugal) and US$100 (double the median income in Luxembourg)[7]. Christian Meyer and Nancy Birdsall use the same lower base of US$10, in 2005 PPP terms, and place the upper limit at $50 (the cut-off between "middle class" and "rich" in Latin America)[8].

- Martin Ravaillon indicates a lower boundary of US$2, at 2005 PPP, and an upper level at US$13 (the 2005 US poverty line). The Asian Development Bank uses the same lower level of US$2 and places the upper one at US$20, at 2005 PPP. Abhijit Banerjee and Esther Duflo place the threshold between US$2 and US$10 daily per capita expenditure, at 1993 PPP, distinguishing between a lower middle class, at between US$2 and US$4, and an upper middle class, at between US$6 and US$10[9].

Comparing middle class levels in developing countries to those of the global middle class, as some of the above do, is viewed as at times distorting, since it does not take sufficiently into account existing differences. Calculations – as noted – should be based on a definition of middle class as made up of persons poor by developed countries standards but having a reasonable amount of disposable income according to the standards of developing countries.

---

[7] H. Kharas, *The Emerging Middle Class in Developing Countries*, Global Development Outlook, Working Paper no. 285, 2010

[8] C. Meyer, N. Birdsall, *New Estimates of India's Middle Class*, Technical Note, Center for Global Development, 2012.

[9] All the above quoted in S. Krishnan, N. Hatekar, "Rise of the New Middle Class in India and Its Changing Structure", *Economic&PoliticalWeekly*, vol. 52, no. 22, 3 June 2017.

Others prefer not to use income- and consumption-based criteria. Devesh Kapur proposes two alternative methods: a) number of persons filing income-tax returns: this was equal in 2011-2012 to 28.7 million (2.3% of the population);16.2% were, however, exempt from paying taxes, thus reducing the total number of taxpayers to around 12.5 million (roughly equivalent to 5-6% of India's households); b) share of Indians with a college degree, equal in 2010 to approximately 50 million[10]. Leela Fernandes makes reference to behavioural measures that take into account the role of social, cultural and economic forces in the construction of class identity[11]. Others use the nature of employment to define middle class, underlining a decline in the previous dominance of government employment and the rise of private sector and self-employed jobs, which would appear to reflect the country's overall change in the social and work fabric. Anirudh Krishna and Devendra Bajpai use the criteria of ownership of transportation assets, placing in the lower middle class owners of a motorcycle or scooter, in the upper middle class owners of a car, and among the rich those possessing both a car and an air conditioner[12]. Finally, Devesh Kapur, Neelanjan Sircar and Milan Vaishnav propose a self-assessment approach based on interviews of over 150,000 households, whose results approximate those that could be reached in an advanced industrial society; i.e. self-identification with middle class is greater at lower- and middle-income levels and tends to decline at higher levels; it is equally higher among urban dwellers and declines in rural areas[13].

---

[10] D. Kapur, "The Middle Class in India: A Social Formation or Political Actor?", in J. Go (ed.), *Political Power and Social Theory*, Emerald Group Publishing Limited, 2010.

[11] L. Fernandes, *India's New Middle Class*, University of Minnesota Press, 2006.

[12] A. Krishna, D. Bajpai, "Layers in Globalizing Society and the New Middle Class India: Trends, Distribution and Prospects", Economic&PoliticalWeekly, 2015.

[13] D. Kapur, N. Sircar, and M. Vaishnav, *The Importance of Being Middle Class in India*, Washington DC, Carnegie Endowment for International Peace, 3 November 2017.

The above criteria are based on long-term observation and the use of different statistical and quantitative analyses. The criteria and reference points used are of importance in circumscribing the broad remit of what can be viewed as middle class in India, but their quantitative parameters are at times inevitably dated and struggle to keep pace with more recent economic and societal developments: placing them in context with data pertaining to the present situation may be helpful. GDP per capita is at US$1,700 (or US$6,600 in PPP terms), less than half of China's, and 80% of the population are behind [below?] this line. According to Thomas Piketty and others, in 2014 around 78 million Indians had an income in excess of US$3,150, and only 1% made more than US$20,000 (US$75,000 in PPP). PPP criteria provide a more realistic comparison between otherwise disparate economic conditions and are widely utilised; some caution should be used, however. PPP allows for the offsetting of the relative importance of factors such as infrastructure, health, education, social facilities etc., that make up the collective wealth of a country, but is often unable to fully reflect the impact of "global" consumer patterns in the composition of real disposable income. An Indian middle-class consumer will have a comparative advantage in respect of his US counterpart in many areas; when buying Nike shoes or subscribing to Netflix, he will be using not PPP, but "real" dollars, just like him, with a very different impact on the actual size of their respective disposable incomes[14].

Size

Establishing the size of the new middle class is equally elusive, and is influenced not only by statistical analysis, but equally by aspirational considerations and political priorities. That the last decade has seen a considerable increase is undeniable, but actual numbers and expected trends tend to differ according to the angle from which they are taken, be that of a projected increase

---

[14] "India's missing middle class", *The Economist*, 11 January 2019.

in the consumer market base, as a tool to encourage further domestic and international investment, or that of governments keen to present the image of a country moving away fast from the poverty trap and acquiring the character and strength of a mature and diverse society.

The 2007 McKinsey report once again provides a good reference point. According to its estimation, the middle class should grow from around 50 million to 583 million by 2025, equal to 41% of total urban population. Figures vary widely, however, as indicated in the table below[15].

TAB. 3.1 – VARIOUS DEFINITIONS OF THE "INDIAN MIDDLE CLASS"

Source	Size	Year	Definition
Beinhocker et al. (2007)	50 million	2005	House hold with disposable income between ₹200,000-₹1,000,000 per year (approx. 11-$55/day and $4,200-$21,000/year)
McKinsey Global Institute (2010)	32 million (households)	2008	Households with disposable income between ₹200,000-₹1,000,000 per year
Singh (2005)	113 million 250 million	1992-1993 1998-1999	Broadest middle class: households income greater than ₹35,000 per year (in 1998-1999 rupees)
Sridharan (2004)	55-248 million	1998-1999	By household income - Elite: > ₹140,000/yr. - Expanded: > ₹105,001/yr. - Broadest: > ₹70,001/yr.

---

[15] D. Kapur, N. Sircar, and M. Vaishnav (2017).

Desai (2008)	7% of all households 11% of all households	1983 1999-2000	Proportion of households with consumption expenditure above ₹60,000 (in 1999 rupees)
Government of India (2012)	28.7 million	2011-2012	Number of people filing tax returns
Shukla (2010)	4.5 million households 10.7 million households 28.4 million households	1995-1996 2001-2002 2099-2010	Income between ₹0.2-₹1.0 million
Asian Development Bank (2010)	224 million (lower middle class) 45 million (middle-middle class) 5 million (upper middle class)	2005	$2-$4 (PPP) $4-$10 (PPP) $10-$20 (PPP)
Kharas (2010)	5-10% of all households	2010	$10-$100
	70 million	2012	Income between $10-$50
India Human Development Survey (IHDS), 2011-2012 Round	40% of all households	2014	Income between ₹55,000-₹88,000
Birdsall (2015)	2.6% of all households	2015	Income between $10-$50
Pew Research Center (2015)	3% of all households	2015	Income between $10.01-$20 (2011 PPP)

The differences reflect the way in which middle class identity is related to contemporary Indian society. If we define a middle-class household in conventional Western terms, i.e. owning a house/flat, having a car or a scooter, a television and air conditioner, enjoying regular holidays and eating out from time to time, numbers shrink considerably: according to a government survey quoted by *The Economist*, under 3% of all households qualified for this standard in 2012[16]. Knowledge of English is the necessary prerequisite for accessing a developed consumer market, whose message is nearly exclusively in English: roughly 10% of the population are fully conversant in the language, despite what may appear to a superficial observer noting that road signs and hoardings are nearly always in English[17]. Income tax is a typical middle-class obligation: not only just 28.7 million citizens filed an income tax return in 2011-2012, but in the run up to the May 2019 general elections, the Modi government doubled the income tax threshold from Rs. 250,000 to Rs. 500,000[18]. A figure which may be of help in putting further into focus the criteria mentioned earlier.

Despite significant growth in provincial and rural areas, the Indian middle class is predominantly urban, and will be even more so by 2025 as the move towards large cities becomes widespread. The increase in numbers is not accompanied by a fairer distribution of the income and wealth curve, which points to a greater polarisation, with the top 10% of earners becoming richer at the expense of the others: their share of national income, which was 40% in 2000, is now over 55%, while that of lower earners shrunk over the same period from 40% to under 30%. The top 1% account for 22% of national income (against 14% in China), there are 200,000 millionaires and 101 billionaires according to Forbes, and the figure moves up every few months[19]. In terms of overall wealth, India compares with

---

[16] "India's Missing Middle Class"…, cit.

[17] While not as widely spoken as believed, English is the **only** language spoken throughout India (unlike Hindi and the regional idioms) and even a rudimentary knowledge is sufficient to read and understand hoardings and road signs. Which is why they are in English. Cfr. A. Armellini, *If the Elephant Flies: India Confronts the Twenty-First Century*, New Delhi, Har Anand, 2012.

[18] A. Kazmin, "Will Narendra Modi "giveaways" woo voters?", *Financial Times*, 8 February 2019.

[19] "India's Missing Middle Class"…, cit.

Switzerland and Korea; its market is heavily segmented, both in terms of regional distribution and of consumer potential, and even though it is relatively small in absolute terms, given the size of the country's population it compares favourably with those of large developed countries.

Caste and Class: An India-Specific Conundrum?

It is difficult for anyone – and especially for a non-Indian – to fully grasp the nature of caste and its link to the intricacies of Indian society. As Susan Bayly writes: "Any quest for a single model or formula of caste (is) a deeply frustrating experience"[20]. Caste is not a subject of the present study and will not be dealt with *in extenso*, but it should be borne in mind that it remains an important component of the historical, cultural and political identity of the country, criss-crossing in various ways its entire social fabric. Class – as the term itself tells – is by definition separate from caste, and economic development tends to gradually make the middle class independent from traditional caste categorisation. Yet it continues to play a significant role in middle-class composition, apparently to a greater extent than religion. According to Sandhya Khrishnan and Neeraj Hatekar, in 2011-2012 the new middle class was composed in roughly equal terms of 45.1% Muslims and 50.3% Hindus, among which upper castes accounted for 63.7% and lower castes for 29.2%[21]. Middle class is no longer a predominantly urban phenomenon as wealth moves beyond larger provincial centres to include rural areas, where caste has scarcely lost its relevance. Changes in its impact will take place, but not as fast as some would like to believe, and not necessarily in ways in accordance with the tenets of Western socio-economic analysis[22].

---

[20] Susan Bayly, *Caste, Society, and Politics in India*, quoted in A. Armellini (2012).

[21] S. Krishnan, N. Hatekar (2017). Percentages and figures are criticised by other studies, however.

[22] For a more detailed analysis of caste structure and problems, see: *Un paese a più*

The McKinsey report and others discussed above look, with only few exceptions, at the middle class largely in terms of its economic potential and consequent implications for market expansion and take only indirectly account of the impact in terms of societal organisation. Figures veer on occasion too much on the optimistic side[23], and the recent rollercoaster swings in the economy have given rise to concern, but even taking into consideration the possibility of a substantial pruning the opportunities remain considerable. The very rich already sustain a market in luxury high-end products that compares favourably with that of the industrialised world: a casual observer could be swayed by the Armani and Gucci malls sprouting all over or by the fact that Rolls Royce and Lamborghini sell in a matter of days their annual allotment of cars, despite import duties in excess of 100%. But it is the aspirational pull of the lower segment of the less well-to-do, coupled with a geographical distribution that makes hitherto more peripheral areas of the country a valid business proposition, that provide greater scope for investors, both domestic and international, despite high duties and an impossible bureaucracy. It remains to be seen if market growth will succeed in accelerating the trickle-down effect in the economy that should – eventually – turn India into a less unequal society but, seen from the angle of money and markets, the middle class is a player of increasing importance and the correlation with caste has a subsidiary role.

If the question is: can the new middle class be a crucial factor in accelerating economic growth, but not necessarily ensuring a more equal distribution of wealth, the answer is probably yes, with the proviso of avoiding the risk of falling into the all-too-common Indian trap of hyperbole. It is at the core of Narendra Modi's bid for continued power, and there are elements of fragility.

---

strati, quoted in A. Armellini, *L'elefante ha messo le ali. L'India del XXI secolo*, Milan, UBE, 2013.

[23] www.ibe.org is a daily business information service of the India Brand Equity Foundation, run by the Ministry of Commerce, which is especially rich in positive and at times over the top information

Being Middle Class Under Modi

Modi presented himself as a moderniser capable of interpreting the ambition of those sections of the population that no longer felt adequately represented by traditional parties and were tired of Congress-dominated coalitions, weakened by the gradual eclipse of the Nehru-Gandhi dynasty. Having succeeded in putting aside – Blair style – the entire old leadership of his party he projected a message capable of going beyond the traditional support base of the BJP and of cutting across traditional divides. It was a message directed to an urban middle class attracted by the promise of a new impetus to economic reforms that had been initiated by the Manmohan Singh governments and stalled halfway, re-launching privatisation of state-owned behemoths, cutting red tape and in general terms according priority to business interests. To an aspirational rural one as well, which was given the promise of a massive increase in infrastructure projects, together with a short-cut passport towards modernity through flagship programmes such as the latrines in every village scheme and the promotion of micro-banking for agriculture. In the first instance, the message appeared essentially caste-neutral, but in the second the correlation between caste and class continued to carry weight. Underlining his origins as the son of a lower-caste *chaiwallah,* proved important for Modi not only in securing the hard core of his own caste-based support, but equally in promoting a new consciousness through which lower-caste would be seen as not incompatible with, but rather conducive to middle class inclusion. As proved by himself.

Modi's message has been twofold. On the one hand, announcing grand programmes for domestic reform, launching a more aggressive foreign policy and asserting a great-power role for India, keen to establish privileged links in the region and moving away from an obsessive inferiority complex towards China. On the other, pushing a nationalist agenda with occasional jingoistic overtones that represent to some extent his inner beliefs, as someone who has been a lifelong member of the RSS[24] but is equally, if not more, important in keeping the allegiance of segments of the population less directly exposed to the benefits of economic development. And which are more susceptible to an intolerant Hindu message, necessarily based on caste identity as a means of personal realisation. Juggling between the two is at the basis of his strategy to consolidate support, in conjunction or contrast as the need may arise, and as a function of his ability to deliver in economic terms. It allows him, among others, to play a delicate game with respect to the support of the Muslim middle class, which went beyond expectations at the 2014 elections (to the expense of Congress) but was then reversed by concerns over the upswing in nationalist and communal propaganda, in parallel with the worsening of the economic scene.

The urban middle class continues to be a dominant force in wealth distribution and is crucial in voting terms: in the 2011 census it accounted for 32% of the population and for 60% of GDP, which by 2030 should reach 70%[25]. Support can be fickle, however, as it is based more on economic expectations than on traditional party and political affiliations. Based on a highly effective communications strategy, the Modi government has boasted of a number of successes, from the sea-change in the practices of a somnolent and corrupt bureaucracy to the introduction of long-delayed administrative reforms and the creation of new infrastructure, such as airport expansion and the completion of the long-heralded "golden quadrangle" of state-of-the art highways.

Yet the promise of jump-starting the process of modernisation, bringing an inefficient banking system up to standard and making India more open to foreign investment, among other things, has run into many hitches and remains at best

---

[24] Rashtryia Swayamesevak Sangh, extremist nationalist organisation founded in 1925 by K.B. Hedgewar, and partially fashioned after the Italian youth fascist organisation Opera Balilla, see A. Armellini (2013).
[25] McKinsey Global Institute, *India's Global Awakening: Building Inclusive Cities, Sustaining Economic Growth*, McKinsey&Company, April 2010.

incomplete. After having edged up over China's, India's GDP declined to 6.7% in 2018, and the present forecast of a 7.2% increase in 2019 is open to doubt[26]. The interplay between the quest for economic efficiency and the pull of nationalist intransigence has produced some unwarranted outcomes. A massive demonetisation programme, announced as a means to wipe out corruption and clean up inefficient trading practices, proved questionable in economic policy terms and created havoc in the country, especially damaging the smaller "informal" trading sector and proving largely insufficient at combating money laundering and smuggling. The introduction of a country-wide unified VAT-type indirect taxation system was badly needed and had been announced – and delayed – for more than ten years; its botched-up introduction showed that India still has a long way to go to reach acceptable levels of administrative efficiency and has been taking an inordinate amount of time to come fully into effect.

Both affected directly the sectors of the population on which the BJP traditionally, and Modi's BJP especially, relied as a core basis of support and this, coupled with growing woes in the general economic situation, has sent ripples of increasing dimension through an electorate that could start to look again at the prospects of an opposition buoyed by what appears to be a – finally – rejuvenated Congress, despite its continuing inability to turn a definitive leaf on the Nehru-Gandhi hold on the party. Sonia Gandhi's rumoured illness has kept her out of the limelight for some time; Rahul Gandhi's attempts at becoming an actual leader have been brave and not entirely convincing but the appearance on the scene of his sister Pryianka – who in determination and looks brings to mind her grandmother Indira – could prove to be a game changer.

Recent upsets in regional elections could be seen not only in light of the many unrealised promises of swift change, but also in light of the continued influence of caste in determining voter

---

[26] P. Sakpal, *Election Muddies India's Outlook*, 5 February 2018; www.omfif.org

orientation. This appeared to be especially evident in Uttar Pradesh, where caste still rules the roost, but equally in other more socially articulate states, where it proved an additional, and at times insufficiently accounted for, factor in determining an unexpected result. Modi's reactions to what were until recently hard to imagine difficulties have been uneven. He has forced the resignation of a competent and internationally respected governor of the Central Bank, Urjit Patel, who resisted his attempt to bend the bank's independence to his short-term political exigencies and replaced him with a more pliant former civil servant, Shatikanta Das, giving rise to concerns over the longer-term financial stability of the country. Faced with growing criticism in the media, he has tried to introduce limitations in the use of social media and is apparently considering the introduction of some form of censorship on Internet access, following but not quite replicating the Chinese example[27].

The freer hand given to Hindu extremists both within and outside his party's power base has led some to believe that the government may be casting a blind eye on the increase in communal strife, as a means to shore up its hard-core Hindu support in the run up to the polls, making full use of the caste identity card to the detriment of the broader message to middle class voters; not to mention the issue of the Muslim middle-class vote. Things could get out of hand and special attention is necessary not only in relation to the Indian domestic scene, but equally to possible international implications[28]. If push comes to shove, some believe that Modi could fall back on his deeply-felt beliefs, putting tactical considerations on a backburner and placing caste at the forefront of his strategy, over class (and especially middle class). They see a first element of such a development in the recent government decision, following upheavals in Rajasthan, to extend the job-reservation policy designed for

---

[27] V. Goel, "India Proposes Chinese-Style Internet Censorship", *The New York Times*, 14 February 2019.
[28] Which could reverberate negatively also on the ongoing controversy regarding the two Italian marines.

underprivileged groups to some higher but impoverished upper castes; a move that could be seen as a subtle way of instrumentalising caste divisions in order to reaffirm the supremacy of political decision-making, while at the same time negating caste's traditional foundation. I disagree with Ashok Malik's statement that "the principal appeal of Modi in contemporary India is not religion, or caste o even hyper-nationalism. It is class"[29]. His appeal appears to be based instead on a combination of all the above elements, which play differently according to the situation and components of society involved, and their interrelation is at the basis of his political strategy's success.

The Modi promise of rapid change and accelerated modernisation has been partly stifled: India has a strong international profile, an increasingly powerful army and growing ambitions, but its 500 million-plus poor confine it still to a partly third-world condition, in conflict with its advanced first-world other self. Congress may point to its decades-long record of past development, stronger in social awareness than in economic accomplishment. Modi can stress the undoubted impact his government has had on the internal attitude and the external perception of India as an elephant finally on an accelerated ascendant slope. Hiding but not entirely removing the stain of its intolerant other self. As noted by Pavan Varma[30], the new Indian middle class is presently driven by self-realisation and greed more than by ideology or social and political commitment, and a downswing in the overall economic picture could negatively impact Modi's legacy and increase the attractiveness of a more socially inclusive message coming from a Pryianka-led coalition.

Conclusion

The middle class is a growing player in the Indian social and political scene, and yet remains elusive in many respects. It

---

[29] A. Malik, The India that Made Modi, ECFR.
[30] Ibid.

has a major role in economic terms: its numbers, geographical distribution and sociological variety provide for a market both diversified in quality and range and increasing in volume, irrespective of substantial differences in comparison with advanced industrialised countries. Its ability to generate the trickle-down effect needed to make India a less unequal society remains open to question, as does its capacity to become part of a realistic fiscal structure. From the angle of political consensus, the role of the middle class remains intertwined with that of caste, in ways that may be changing but will not disappear soon, or easily. This is a trait that is difficult to explain in full with Western eyes and should be accepted as an intrinsic and inherently "different" component of Indian identity.

4. Inequality: Global India's Domestic Bottleneck?

Nicola Missaglia

India, home to almost one fifth of the world's population, is no stranger to inequality. Over the last decades, the impressive growth story that has been transforming the country into a major regional and international player since the early 2000s has often overshadowed the news about this domestic challenge. However, an increasing number of studies assess that India's sustained economic growth, spurred by the "first generation" reforms in the 1990s, has not necessarily been matched by a comparable increase in the equality of wealth and opportunities for all of its citizens. Although India is still home to one of the world's largest numbers of people living below the international poverty line of 1.90 dollars per day[1], it has made momentous progress in reducing poverty, pulling more than 270 million people out of extreme indigence over the last decade[2]. Yet India today remains a country of high inequality. Even more worryingly, the levels of inequality in India are not only high: they have been increasing at a speedy pace since the 1990s, in coincidence with the beginning of deregulation policies and economic liberalisation in those years, and in concomitance with the country's soaring growth during the last three decades. Data

---

[1] "India has highest number of people living below poverty line: World Bank", *Business Today*, 3 October 2016.
[2] "271 million people moved out of poverty in India: UN Development Programme", *Hindustan Times*, 21 September 2018.

made available by recent research also show that the gains of growth have been unevenly distributed across Indian states and different sections of the population. This chapter tries to give an overview of the main dimensions of inequality and regional disparities in India today. It argues that if Indian policymakers don't address both of these challenges swiftly, they could become major drivers of socio-political instability and centrifugal trends in the country, posing a serious risk to India's achievements and threatening to jeopardise the country's ambition to become a leading power.

Rich and Poor: Inequality in India

For years, many observers have downplayed the importance of inequality, and of its impact for the future of rapidly growing economies, because of the argument that inequality is a natural by-product of rapid growth. As far as India is concerned, until recently – with few notable exceptions[3] – the study of domestic inequality has been given inadequate attention, too. One reason for this is that India's outstanding progress in reducing multidimensional poverty since its economy began to accelerate in the early 2000s has often grabbed the headlines. And indeed, according to the latest available data from the United Nations Development Programme, between 2005/2006 and 2015/2016 India almost halved the incidence of multidimensional poverty, from 54.7% to 27.5%, pulling a total of 271 million citizens out of extreme poverty over the ten-year period[4].

Another reason for the scant attention that has been given to overall inequality in India, is that here – differently from most countries – the level of inequality is not usually measured

---

[3] See D. Gupta, *The Caged Phoenix. Can India Fly?*, Paolo Alto CA, Stanford University Press, 2010. Also see and see Oxfam, "Widening Gaps", India Inequality Report 2018.

[4] *271 million fewer poor people in India*, United Nations Development Programme, Multidimentional Poverty Index 2018.

by its income dimension (also due to the limited information available), but by consumption expenditure data: and in fact, according to these data, consumption expenditure inequality[5] in India appears to be lower than income inequality, and lower than in most other developing countries. This has even led some to claim that, by international standards, India can be considered a low-inequality country[6], although consumption and income inequality do not necessarily have a one-to-one correspondence[7].

Last but not least, for several years the lack of reliable data and information has made it more difficult to assess how the gains of growth in India have been distributed among different sections of the population. This was not the case as far as the impact of economic growth on poverty reduction in the country is concerned: and unsurprisingly, much of the public debate over the last decades – both in India and abroad – has been focusing on this latter, undeniably positive, dimension of India's rise.

However, also thanks to the use of new sources of data that had long been unavailable or underestimated – e.g. tax data, national accounts or household surveys – more recent work has made it possible to better assess how wealth and income growth is distributed across India's population. Not by chance, for the first time in years the issue of economic inequality was brought into the mainstream political debate by the 2019 general election campaign, whereas previous campaigns had mainly focused on economic growth and not on its repartition[8].

---

[5] See M.A. Aguiar and M. Bils, *Has Consumption Inequality Mirrored Income Inequality?*, NBER Working Paper no. 16807, The National Bureau of Economic Research, February 2011.

[6] See examples quoted by Himanshu, "Inequality in India", *Seminar*, no. 625, 2015.

[7] D. Krueger and F. Perri, "Has Consumption Inequality Mirrored Income Inequality? Evidence and Theory", National Bureau of Economic Research, NBER Working Paper no. 9202, September 2002.

[8] P. Bhattacharya, "Why income inequality in India may be fuelling populist politics", *LiveMint*, 8 January 2019; also see "Tackling inequality in India. Is the 2019

New evidence shows that, despite sustained growth rates over a prolonged period of time, India today is still a highly unequal country. Moreover, available information suggests that inequality in India has been witnessing a swiftly rising trend over the last three decades (Figure 4.1), unlike most countries that started with high inequality and then saw it decline or only slowly increase[9]. This means that, for the time being, the gains of the country's spectacular growth have been unevenly distributed among its citizens and have failed to translate into increased welfare for all, both rich and poor. In a recent report, Oxfam rightly pointed out that "the welfare of the population is however dependent not only on the growth of the economy but also on its distributional outcomes"[10].

Studying the extent and trends of inequality is key to understanding the growth trajectories of an emerging and fast growing market economy like India's. If not properly addressed, inequality might create dangerous bottlenecks in the path of the country's impressive growth story. This section examines the rising incidence of income or wealth inequality in India[11], and

election campaign up to the challenge?", World Inequality Index, WID.world Issue Brief 2019/2, March 2019.

[9] See "Widening Gaps"…, cit.

[10] See "Public Good or Private Wealth?" Oxfam Inequality Report 2018. The India Story. The report points out that "The most credible measure of inequality in the country is based on the consumption surveys of the NSSO. Based on these, the Gini of consumption expenditure as measured by the National Sample Survey (NSS) consumption expenditures surveys report a rise in consumption inequality from 0.32 in 1993-94 to 0.38 in 2011-12 for urban areas. Corresponding estimates of Gini of consumption expenditure in rural areas is 0.26 in 1993-94 to 0.29 in 2011-12. On income inequality, the latest data on income inequality is available from the India Human Development Survey (IHDS) reports which show income inequality in India in 2011-12 at 0.55, up from 0.53 in 2004-05 which puts India among the high inequality countries (B.G. Desai et al., "Ichnology of the Early Cambrian Tal Group, Nigalidhar Syncline, Lesser Himalaya, India", *Ichnos*, vol. 17, no. 4, 2010, pp. 233-245). But even on wealth inequality, India is among the most unequal countries in the world."

[11] For an in-depth analysis of the rising levels of consumption inequality in India, see "Public Good or Private Wealth?"… cit., pp. 21-32.

gives a brief overview of the horizontal dimensions of inequality in access to basic services and opportunities across gender, caste, religious affiliation and location.

FIG. 4.1 - GINI INDEX OF INEQUALITY IN INDIA

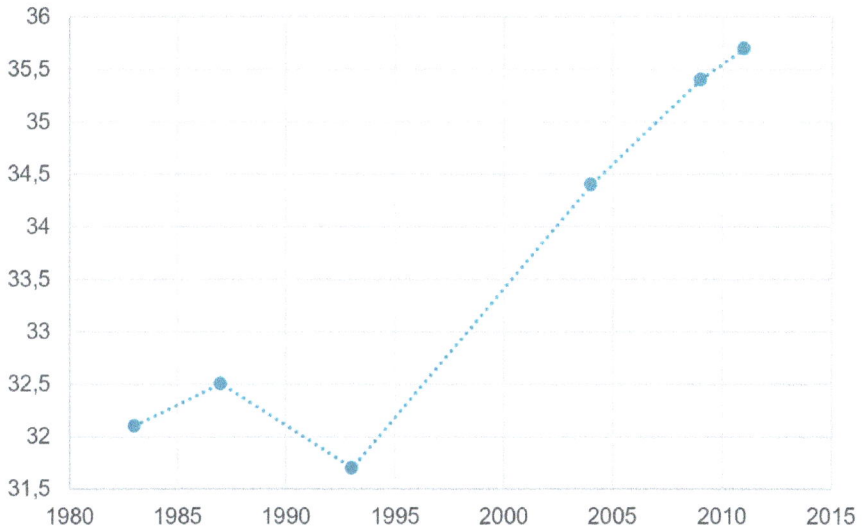

Source: ISPI processing of World Bank data

Inequality in income and wealth

Inequality in wealth and income distribution is not new to India. However, while overall average wealth and income in India have been rising over the last decades (Figure 4.2), it seems that not all Indians have shared this growth.

Fig. 4.2 - Evolution of average income in India (1988-2017)

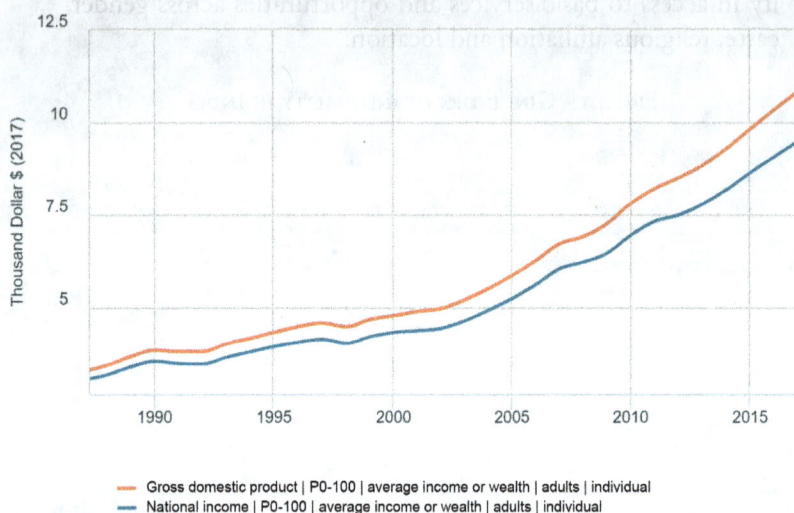

Gross domestic product | P0-100 | average income or wealth | adults | individual
National income | P0-100 | average income or wealth | adults | individual

Source: Data and computing provided
by World Inequality Database (www.wid.world)

In fact, the gap between rich and poor Indians remains extremely high today. On the one hand, despite an undeniable success in multidimensional poverty reduction, India is still an overwhelmingly poor country, where only a small share of Indian adults (0.6%) has net worth over 100,000 dollars, while 91% of the total adult population (850 million) has individual wealth below 10,000 dollars[12]. On the other hand, available data confirm that polarisation between rich and poor citizens in India is patent, and indeed increasing.

---

[12] Ibid.

FIG. 4.3 - INCOME INEQUALITY IN INDIA (1988-2015)

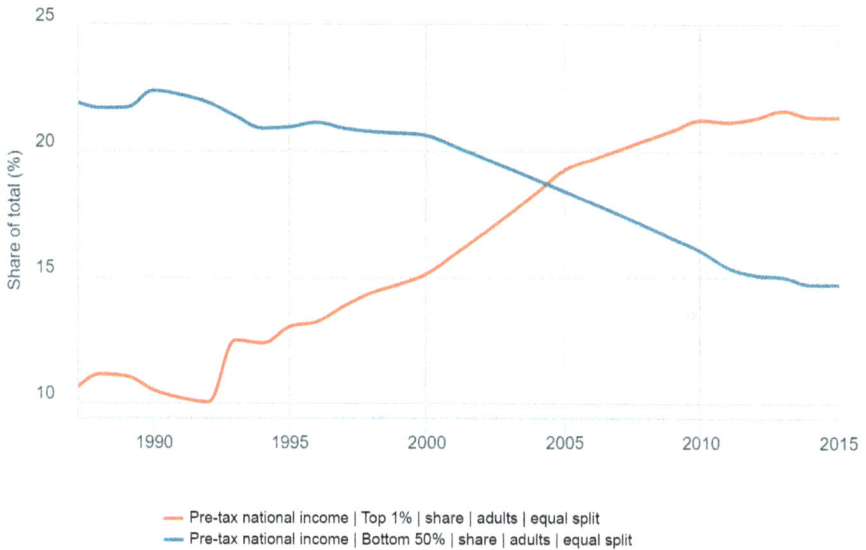

Source: Data and computing provided
by World Inequality Database (www.wid.world)

If we focus on a time series, inequality in income and wealth in India has been rising steadily over the last three decades. The share of income earned by the richest 1% of India's population has been soaring over this period of time, whereas average earnings by the bottom 50% of the population have gradually declined. In 1988 the total share of pre-tax national income earned by the top 1% of the population (Figure 4.3) was 11.1% and that earned by the bottom 50% of Indians 21.7%. Almost thirty years later (latest data available 2015) this proportion was reversed despite demographic growth, with the top 1% holding a 21.3% share and the bottom half just a 14.7% share. Interestingly, the beginning of this divergence coincided with the liberalisation of the country's economy in the mid-1980s and early 1990s, meaning that the policies put in place may have unleashed GDP growth and average income growth (total population), but failed to trigger comparable income growth rates among the bottom income groups of Indians.

Consistently with this picture, since the early 2000s the gap of income distribution between a rich minority and a poor majority has been widening, showing that economic growth and deregulation have clearly benefitted some Indians more than others. As Oxfam points out, this is not surprising since "the rise in the shares of top incomes in India has also been faster than most countries and country groups", while the poorest sections of the country's population have worsened their position. Indeed, recent research shows that not only the income of the richest 1% of Indians grew at more than 7% per year since the beginning of this century, but also that even compared to all-India's average income growth over the same time period (4.7% per year, full population), the average incomes of the bottom 50% and middle 40% sections of the population have grown less than half as fast, at a 2% rate[13].

Divergence in wealth has been increasing, too. Figure 4.4 shows that since the early 1980s, and especially in the post-deregulation decades, the share of wealth held by India's richest citizens has been growing at a constant pace, gradually eclipsing the share of the bottom half of the population, whose wealth on the contrary has been declining. Looking at the time series as shown in this figure, in 1981 the top 1% of India's population held 12.5% of total net personal wealth, the top 10% held 45%, whereas the bottom 50% of Indians held 10.9% of the total and the middle 40% held 44.1%. Thirty years later, in 2012, the gap between the richest share of the population and the poorest share had widened considerably: whereas the top 1% and the middle 40% of Indians now held more or less one third each of

---

[13] L. Chancel and T. Piketty, "Indian income inequality, 1922-2015: From British Raj to Billionaire Raj?", WID.world Working Paper Series no. 2017/11, World Inequality Database, November 2017; and "Tackling inequality in India. Is the 2019 election campaign up to the challenge?"..., cit.; also see M. Sharma, "Thomas Piketty Has a Point About India's Inequality", Bloomberg Quint, 10 October 2017.

total net personal wealth (30.7% and 30.8% respectively, meaning that the richest 1% had increased their wealth by almost 20 points and the middle 40% decreased theirs by almost 15), the top 10% increased their wealth to 62.8% (+17%), and the bottom 50% had almost halved their share to 6.4%.

FIG. 4.4 - WEALTH INEQUALITY IN INDIA (1961-2012)

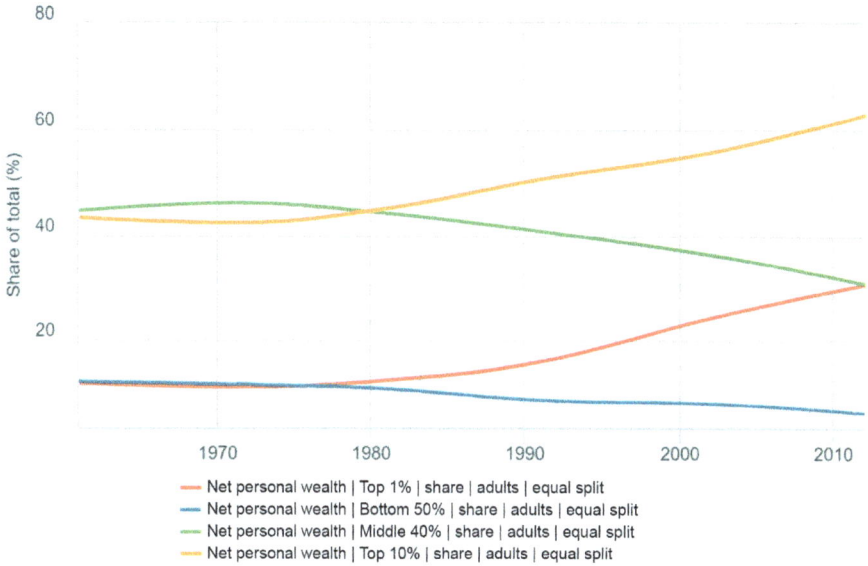

Source: Data and computing provided
by World Inequality Database (www.wid.world)

According to even more recent data provided by Oxfam, the gap has widened even further. Today, India's richest 10% of the population holds 77.4% of total national wealth: a contrast that is even more evident for the top 1% that holds 51.53% of total wealth, whereas the bottom 60% of Indians own just 4.8%. Today, the wealth of India's top 9 billionaires is equivalent to the wealth owned by the bottom 50% of the population[14].

---

[14] "Public Good or Private Wealth?"..., cit.

In the shorter term, recent figures show that throughout 2018 the wealthiest 1% of Indians increased their wealth by 39%, whereas the bottom 50% increased theirs only by a gloomy 3%. The same year, the total wealth of Indian billionaires – whose number in 2018 reached 119 individuals – crossed the 400-billion-dollar threshold for the first time, rising from 325.5 billion dollars in 2017 to 440.1 billion dollars in 2018 (INR 30807 billion): higher than the total Union Budget of India for the fiscal year 2018-2019, which was at INR 24,422 billion. Also, the annual increase of the total wealth owned by the 119 Indian billionaires – an increase of 114.6 billion dollars or INR 8022 billion – can be compared to the combined (centre and states) direct tax revenue of the country in 2016-2017, INR 8621 billion[15].

Several studies published in recent years have pointed out that the rise in income and wealth inequality India has witnessed over the last three decades has no precedent in recent history. The Gini wealth coefficient, as elaborated by Credit Suisse in its *Global Wealth Report 2018*, also confirms this trend. In fact, the coefficient in India rose from 81.2% in 2008 to 85.4% in 2018, where 100% would denote perfect inequality and zero perfect equality.

Horizontal inequality

Inequality also has several non-income dimensions. These can range from poor access to basic public services (e.g. education, health, nutrition, transportation) to an individual's affiliation (e.g. gender, religion, location or, in the case of India, caste). Of course, indicators from these dimensions may overlap or intersect, though not necessarily, with wealth and income dimensions of inequality, or even directly affect the share of income of an individual belonging to one group, if compared to an individual from another group. As elsewhere in the world, in India some groups of people more than others are affected

---

[15] "Public Good or Private Wealth?"…, cit.

by the consequences of inequality[16]. And although exceptions exist, your gender, your caste, your religion or where you are born are likely to directly affect how much you earn, and how many opportunities you are given as a person.

Women

In India, women and men experience the impact of inequality differently. For example, in 2018, an Indian woman was paid on average 19% less than her male counterparts for carrying out the same work[17]. While this figure is still high, in this specific case gender pay gap figures in India have been improving in recent years: in 2011-2012 the national gap was 34%[18], although in 2018 it was more or less the same (20%)[19]. Interestingly, the gender pay gap also varies considerably across Indian states: as per the latest available data, the gap can reach percentages as high as 63% (Bihar), 48% (Chhattisgarh and Assam), 45% (Himachal Pradesh) or 44% (Kerala and Rajasthan), and percentages that don't exceed 9% in Uttarakhand (India's state with the lowest gap), or 10% in Punjab and 15% in Uttar Pradesh[20]. Moreover, these figures describe wage gaps in the formal sector, in a country where the informal economy is still overwhelmingly predominant (around 80%), in spite of the fact that recent governments have increased efforts to tackle this problem, even with controversial measures such as the November 2016 demonetization.[21] Although reliable data lack information for wage inequality in the informal sector, it is safe to assume that here the gender pay gap and disparities in access to decent employment opportunities might be even wider.

---

[16] "Tackling inequality in India. Is the 2019 election campaign up to the challenge?"..., cit.
[17] "Gender pay gap high in India: Men get paid Rs 242 every hour, women earn Rs 46 less", *The Economic Times*, 7 March 2019.
[18] "Public Good or Private Wealth?"..., cit.
[19] "Gender pay gap scenario daunting in India, women get paid 20% less than men", *The Economic Times*, 7 March 2018.
[20] B. Varkkey and R. Korde, "Gender Pay Gap in the Formal Sector: 2006 – 2013", Wage Indicator Data Report, September 2013.
[21] R. Paramahamsa, "Demonetisation: To Deify or Demonise?", Union Budget 2017-2018, Government of India

Fig. 4.5 - Female labour force participation
in India (1990-2018)

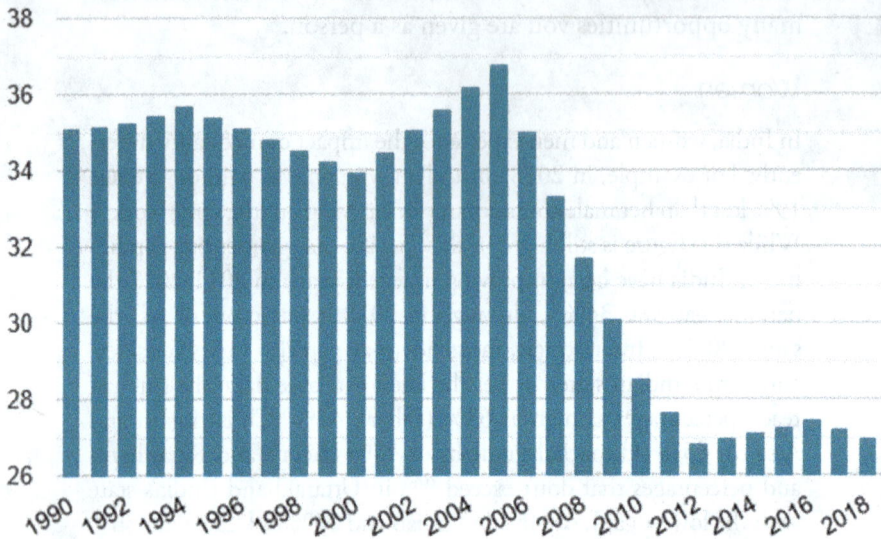

Source: World Bank data, computing provided by TheGlobalEconomy.com

In general, India still performs poorly on the Global Gender
Gap Index and, beyond income inequality, the gap is widening.
If in 2006 India ranked 98th on the World Economic Forum's
Global Gender Gap Index, it lost ten positions in 2018, ranking
108th (out of 144) and 125th (out of 188) on the United Nations
Development Programme's Gender Inequality Index. India's performance is behind that of its neighbours, like Bangladesh and
China. Moreover, with declining female labour force participation,
it looks like the country's growth story has left women behind[22]:
female labour force participation rates in India fell from 35.1% in
1990 to 26.97 in 2018 (Figure 4.5)[23]. Neither the increasing participation of women in education, nor agricultural mechanisation

---

[22] "Public Good or Private Wealth?"…, cit.
[23] See "India: Female labor force participation", TheGlobalEconomy.com

can fully explain this steep decline[24]. Last but not least, according to Oxfam figures, even among India's billionaires, the gender gap is still wide. In the list of India's 119 billionaires there are only 9 women, who hold just 7.5% of total billionaire wealth[25].

Marginalised groups

Since independence, India has made significant gains in the reduction of historic disparities among social groups. Castes were officially abolished by India's 1950 Constitution, and reservation policies and other affirmative measures have been put in place over the decades – even recently[26] – to increase opportunities for the poor and marginalised groups, and reduce discrimination. Today, India's President is a Dalit, and the country's re-elected Prime Minister Narendra Modi's humble background is a well-known fact: a former *chaiwalla* in Gujarat, he made it to the high tables of New Delhi's central power. In recent years, Indian governments have made considerable efforts to harness modern technology for the benefit of disadvantaged citizens, e.g. through the introduction of digital welfare schemes like the so-called JAM Trinity[27], or the implementation of specific pension schemes for informal workers[28].

Although these efforts are important, sizeable inequalities among religious groups and castes in India continue to exist, and intersect with wealth inequalities. Indeed, according to reports published both by India's government[29] and by advocacy groups[30],

[24] C.P. Chandrasekhar and J. Ghosh, *Growth, employment patterns and inequality in Asia: A case study of India*, ILO Asia-Pacific Working Paper Series, International Labor Organization, January 2015.
[25] See "Public Good or Private Wealth?"…, cit.
[26] "Modi govt approves 10 per cent reservation for poor in general category", *The Times of India*, 7 January 2019.
[27] S. Ravi, *Is India Ready to JAM?*, The Brookings Institution, 27 August 2018.
[28] "Unorganised workers can now subscribe to Rs 3,000 monthly pension scheme at common service centres", *The Economic Times*, 17 February 2019.
[29] "Sachar Committee Report", Ministry of Minority Affairs, Government of India, 2006.
[30] "Widening Gaps"…, cit.

religious and caste identities still play a prominent role in the distribution of wealth and income in Indian society, as well as in individual access to basic services such as nutrition, education or health. These inequalities also affect the social mobility and human development outcomes of specific groups of citizens.

In particular, according to data processed by the World Inequality Database, lower castes (Scheduled Castes and Scheduled Tribes) and Muslims – India's largest religious minority group of approximately 200 million people – are still over-represented in the bottom deciles of India's total wealth distribution (bottom 50%) and under-represented in the higher and middle deciles[31]. Whereas the castes classified as Other Backward Castes are evenly represented across all wealth deciles, higher castes (or Forward Castes) are definitely over-represented in the high deciles. Jawaharlal Nehru University Professor Himanshu recently analysed inequality across social and religious groups in India by comparing their share of income and consumption with that of the overall population, where the difference between their share of income and consumption and their population share represents the level of inequality. His research confirms that, relatively to their population shares, Scheduled Castes, Scheduled Tribes, and Muslims have lower shares of income and consumption. Conversely, Forward Castes have higher shares of income and consumption compared to their population shares[32].

Himanshu also points out that despite decades of economic growth, these vulnerable groups have seen their shares of wealth either remain more or less constant over the same period of time or, in the case of Muslims, decline, if compared to their population shares. "Considering the income/consumption/wealth shares of different social groups shows that members of the Scheduled Casts/Tribes had lower shares relative to their population shares in 1993-1994; this continues to be the case even after two decades. Among religious groups, this is the case for Muslims; the

---

[31] "Tackling inequality in India. Is the 2019 election campaign up to the challenge?"…, cit., p. 2.
[32] "Widening Gaps"…, cit., p. 47.

share ratios have declined for this group over the period," he wrote in Oxfam's India Inequality Report 2018[33]. A similar and even bleaker picture of caste/religion-dependent economic inequality emerges if, beyond income and consumption expenditure, the asset shares of these groups are compared to their population shares. This is particularly true for Muslims, and to a lesser extent for Buddhists[34], who have seen their asset share decline over the years, whereas other religious groups (including smaller groups like Christians, Jains and Sikhs) have seen their share of assets increase (See Table 4.1).

TAB. 4.1 - MEASURES OF ASSET INEQUALITY BY RELIGIOUS GROUP

Religious group	Asset share/ Population share	
	2002	2012
Hindu	0.99	1.00
Muslim	0.65	0.57
Christian	1.58	1.67
Sikh	3.27	3.32
Jain	3.52	7.09
Buddhist	0.58	0.57
Others	0.81	0.52

Source: "Widening Gaps", Oxfam Inequality Report 2018, p.49, Author's calculations from the 59th and 70th round of AIDIS

---

[33] "Widening Gaps"…, cit., p. 8

[34] In the case of Buddhists the decline in asset share also depends on the large percentage of Scheduled Castes who have converted to Buddhism over the last decades.

Access to basic services

Inequalities in access to wealth and social inequalities rooted in the historical or cultural marginalisation of certain groups also lead to disparities in the access to basic services. These, in turn, translate into further inequality in the levels of health, nutrition, or education, with a direct impact on the life chances, employment opportunities and social mobility of poorer citizens and disadvantaged groups. As a matter of fact, all of these dimensions are intertwined, and even within disadvantaged groups, phenomena like gender-based discrimination can lead to further exclusion and to the exacerbation of disparities.

Despite momentous progress in poverty reduction, India still lags behind most other countries in hunger and nutrition indicators. The Global Hunger Index 2018 ranks the country 103rd of the 119 that were studied, down three positions from 2017, although in the long term India has managed to improve its standing[35]. With a score of 31.1 – still an improvement if compared to 38.8 in 2000 – India suffers from a level of hunger that the Index describes as "serious". Still today, 42% of children from India's tribal groups are underweight, that is, one and a half times more than non-tribal children. Kids from poor Indian families are three times more likely to die before their first birthday than children from rich families, and a Dalit woman can expect to live almost 14.6 years less than one from a high caste[36].

Also, the decline in malnutrition and hunger prevalence has been slower in disadvantaged groups like Scheduled Castes and Scheduled Tribes, and the imbalance between social groups has hardly changed, although there have been some improvements over the last decade. As Oxfam points out, "this imbalance in the incidence of undernutrition and the slow pace of decline in nutritional deficiencies is rooted in the access to health services. Historically, marginalised groups such as Dalits, tribals and Muslims are disadvantaged not just in the access to wealth but

---

[35] See, "Global Hunger Index 2018", India Country Data.
[36] "Public Good or Private Wealth?"…, cit.

also in the access to basic services, which then leads to lower levels of health, nutrition and education"[37].

Along with socio-cultural and wealth disparities, much of the persistence (or increase) of inequality related to non-income dimensions in India can be attributed to the continued low levels – and low quality – of public spending, and under-investment in basic services. Of course, this is a problem that affects every Indian, but that is likely to have a much greater – even existential – impact on poor and marginalised citizens than on wealthier and more integrated ones. Indeed, despite prospects that India may become "an upper middle-income country by 2030"[38] and the country accounts for one-fifth of the Global Burden of Disease[39], its public spending on health still hovers around little more than 1% of GDP. In this regard, Narendra Modi's recent promise to increase public health spending to 2.5% of GDP by 2025 is a positive sign[40]. For the time being, however, most of the total expenditure for health in India (around 64%)[41] is spent out of pocket by the country's citizens, with a burdensome – if not unsustainable – impact on the finances of their households. As a result, one fifth of the ill in both rural and urban areas deny themselves treatment, where 68% of patients in urban India and 57% in rural areas mention "financial constraints" as the main reason to self-treat without any medical advice. Even more worryingly, millions of Indians every year – 63 million, according to Oxfam – are pushed into poverty as a direct consequence of the costs of healthcare[42]. Strikingly,

---

[37] "Widening Gaps"…, cit., p. 50.

[38] "'We must make India an upper middle-income country by 2030'", *The New Indian Express*, 18 April 2018.

[39] "Global Burden of Disease Study 2017", Institute for Health Metrics and Evaluation, 2017.

[40] "Govt committed to increase India's wealth spending to 2.5 percent of GDP by 2025: Modi"…, cit.

[41] World Bank data, Out-of-pocket expenditure (% of current health expenditure) in India.

[42] "In tangible terms it means that India spends INR 1,112 per person on public health per capita every year. This is less than the cost of a single consultation at the country's top private hospitals or roughly the cost of a pizza at many hotels.

India ranks 145th among 195 countries in terms of quality and accessibility of healthcare, and simultaneously 5th on the Medical Tourism Index[43].

Disparities in access to basic health services in India can also have an impact on the education opportunities for disadvantaged groups, and particularly for women within these groups. Annually, 23 million girls in India drop out of school when they start menstruating because of lack of toilets in school and proper menstrual hygiene management facilities[44]. In this regard, the government's recent decision to scrap the 12% tax on sanitary pads that had been introduced with the GST in 2017 is definitely a welcome move that will help in improving the enrolment of girls in school, as well as their access to decent jobs[45].

Lastly, the access to education itself is still a problem for poorer and marginalised households in India. While in the run-up to the 2019 general election the government committed to increase spending to 6% of GDP by 2022[46], according to the latest available World Bank data (2013), both central and state government spending on education still hovers at 3.8%. According to government data, public spending on education has risen to 4.6% under NDA rule between 2014 and 2019, but is still below the world's average of 4.7% of GDP. In education too, it is women and marginalised groups of citizens (e.g. in rural areas) who pay the highest price for low public spending. According to data provided by India's National Family Health Survey in 2015-2016, girls from rich families (top 20%) in India get an average of nine years of education, while girls from poor families (bottom 20%) get none

---

That comes to INR 93 per month or INR 3 per day. Indians, therefore, have no other choice but to spend out of pocket on health. As a result, 63 million people are pushed into poverty every year." See "Public Good or Private Wealth?"..., cit.

[43] See Medical Tourism Index 2016-2017, Destination Ranking.

[44] "23 Million Women Drop Out Of School Every Year When They Start Menstruating In India", *NDTV*, 28 May 2019.

[45] "India scraps tampon tax after campaign", *BBC*, 21 July 2018.

[46] "India should spend at least 6% of its GDP on education by 2022, advises NITI Aayog", *India Today*, 21 December 2018.

at all. Also, the percentage of children and young people who were never enrolled in school (age group 5-29) in rural areas is double that of urban areas[47].

Regional disparities

Consistently with rising inequality levels in terms of wealth and income distribution among Indian citizens, recent research has found that inter-state disparities in the country have also been widening over the years, even as all-India's economy swelled in absolute size and influence[48]. Although some degree of persisting inequality among Indian states can be seen as a normal consequence of the regional disparities that have existed since independence, the widening divergence between poorer and richer states – accompanied by rising inequality within these states – was more unexpected. And indeed, this comes as a growing concern for both observers and Indian policy-makers[49]. Their concerns are justified for two reasons: firstly, because the outcomes of India's decades-long planning process, also aimed at bridging the gap between different states, are different than expected, meaning that something has gone wrong in the process; secondly, because persisting, actually growing, disparities among Indian states could become a major domestic driver of political instability, and – just like growing inequalities among citizens – translate into an ominous bottleneck on the path of India's amazing growth story.

Recent reports show that, whereas the per capita income levels of wealthier and poorer states witnessed a period of weak convergence between fiscal years 2008 and 2013, over the following five years (2013-2018) the gap widened again, with significant divergence between rich and poor states (Figure 4.6)[50]. In the longer term, inequality measures like the Gini coefficient for per capita income weighted by state population and the inter-state Gini coefficient, show that – just like wealth and income inequality

---

[47] See National Family Health Survey (NFHS-4), India Report 2015-2016.
[48] "States of growth 2.0", CRISIL, 21 January 2019.
[49] "The Gap Within", *The Hindu*, 24 January 2019.
[50] See "States of growth" CRISIL, 7 December 2017.

among citizens – disparities among Indian states have indeed existed since independence: however, if these disparities remained stable until the 1980s, they have been rising more or less constantly since the early 1990s[51].

FIG. 4.6 - REGIONAL DISPARITIES AND GDP PER CAPITA IN INDIA (2012-2017)

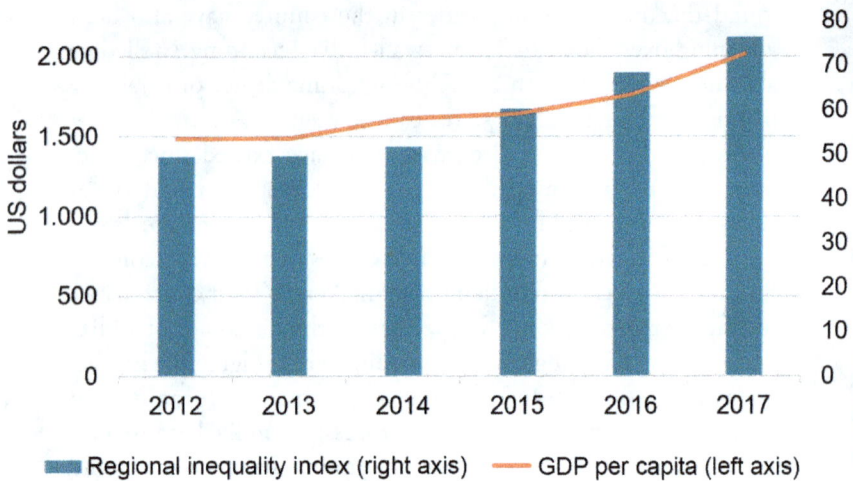

Source: ISPI processing of International Monetary Fund data

This divergence is a consequence of the fact that wealthier states have shown continued strong economic growth rates, whereas poorer states may have experienced isolated years of soaring growth, but still not enough to bridge their per capita income gap with richer states. As the Hindu newspaper recently put it, "they have simply not been able to maintain a healthy growth rate over a sustained period of time"[52]. Thus, poorer states fell behind. For example, according to figures analysed by the rating agency CRISIL for 17 non-special category states, of the eight low-income states

_____

[51] For further details, see Himanshu in "Widening Gaps"…, cit., p. 45.
[52] "The Gap Within"…, cit.

in 2013, only two recorded economic growth rates above the national average until 2018. Conversely, over the same five years, as much as six out of nine high-income states had growth rates that exceeded the national average.

The result of this trend is that, today, India may well be the fastest growing major economy on Earth in terms of absolute size, but disparities between its states and regions are still glaring. This means that, for a number of reasons, the benefits of soaring economic growth are unevenly distributed across the subcontinent's 29 states and 7 union territories, adding to the fact some of India's most populous states are also its poorest – e.g. Uttar Pradesh, with its 200 million citizens. A recent Forbes article put it persuasively: "UP and neighbouring Bihar have a combined population roughly equal to that of the U.S., but a combined GDP less than that of Michigan"[53]. Looking at nominal per capita figures, both of these states have a GDP per capita of less than 1000 dollars, comparable to that of sub-Saharan Africa; whereas the GDP per capita in the National Capital Territory of Delhi (US$5,200), for example, is more than almost five times that of Assam (US$1,200), and more than seven times that of Bihar (US$730). Goa, India's richest state with a population of less than two million, has a per capita GDP on a par with that of Bulgaria, while the state of Manipur, with a comparable population, has a GDP per capita that is more than six time less. Inequalities between Indian cities and the states or territories where they are located can be striking, too. Bangalore, to mention one, is the country's hi-tech capital, hosting technology multinationals and India's top-ranked universities: but Karnataka, its state, has a GDP per capita of 2,600 dollars, comparable to that of Fiji.

As for inflation, significant inter-state differences persist, with the lowest inflation in Odisha at 2.2% and the highest in Kerala at 6%"[54]. Other, non-economic, indicators confirm that disparities among India's states persist on multiple levels: e.g. while the literacy rate in states like Mizoram or Kerala, and the Union Territory

---

[53] S. Babones, "India May Be The World's Fastest Growing Economy, But Regional Disparity Is A Serious Challenge", *Forbes*, 10 January 2018.
[54] "States of growth 2.0"…, cit., pp. 10-11.

of Lakshadweep is over 90%, it is just little more than 60% in Bihar[55].

As stated, India has made outstanding progress in reducing multidimensional poverty, although the country is still a poor country overall, and pockets of poverty are spread across India – with a widening gap between urban and rural areas. However, a fact that deserves to be mentioned in this section is that most of India's poor citizens are not distributed evenly across the country's territory. Rather, the majority of poor Indians are concentrated in some states, namely in India's poorest states. According to recent estimates by the United Nations Development Programme, over half of all multidimensionally poor in India, 196 million people, live in the country's four poorest states today: Bihar, Uttar Pradesh, Madhya Pradesh, and Jharkhand, albeit the latter has made meaningful progress in reducing poverty in recent years[56].

As for why the gap between rich and poor states in India is widening, most of the reports suggest that although states are now the engines of government spending (over 65% of total), most of them are not spending in areas where they ought to, like health, education, infrastructure and irrigation. Of course, the quality of state spending does not only have direct impact on the poorer citizens – who more than others depend on the quality of public services – but also on the states' ability to create a competitive, free marketplace for businesses to flourish over a prolonged period of time, and attract new businesses. Most analysts also point out that other non-economic variables like the strength of state-level institutions and their capacity to uphold the rule of law play a role in regional disparities,

---

[55] "Public Good or Private Wealth?"…, cit.

[56] See "271 million fewer poor people in India", United Nations Development Programme, 20 September 2018, "Across nearly every state, poor nutrition is the largest contributor to multidimensional poverty. Not having a household member with at least six years of education is the second largest contributor. Insufficient access to clean water and child mortality contribute least. Relatively fewer people living in poverty experience deprivations in school attendance – a significant gain". Also see C. Gardìn, "Explaining cross-state earnings inequality differentials in India", WIDER Working Paper 2018/24, United Nations University, February 2018.

too. Last but not least, most analysts suggest that increased cen-tre-state fiscal transfers might have benefitted states that were al-ready performing well – also thanks to variables such as their better quality infrastructure, better fiscal health, the presence of employ-ment-intensive sectors, and the development of commercial and services sectors – rather than poorer and more disadvantaged states which lagged behind in most of these dimensions. Undoubtedly, measures introduced by the Modi government such as the Goods and Services Tax or the highway construction program[57] to enhance domestic connectivity are a good start to reduce internal barriers and help poorer states or regions to benefit from their richer neigh-bours' growth. Similar and even more radical measures aimed at reducing India's regional disparities should be high on the agenda of Modi's re-elected government.

Conclusion. Inequality and India's Quest for Global Leadership

There is much talk today about India being the next global superpower. And rightly so, because India's achievements as a democratic nation, its decades-long growth, its human poten-tial, and last but not least its resolute commitment to a dem-ocratic and rules-based international order[58], are definitely en-bling conditions to become one.

But being a global superpower, or even a regional power, is not only about foreign policy projection, military might and soaring economic growth. Becoming a global superpower also has a domestic dimension: there are number of "internal" is-sues that can either support or hinder a nation's ascent to the status of regional, or even global power. Among the domestic features that can support a nation in its path to global power

---

[57] "Highway construction touched 30 km/day in 2018-19", *The Times of India*, 4 April 2019.
[58] *India is committed to a democratic and rules based international order, says Sushma Swaraj,* Observer Research Foundation, 9 January 2019.

status, there are economic growth, a strong military, a solid industry and demographic power. On the other hand, among the features that can seriously hamper a nation's development and rise, there are "structural" issues such as the lack of natural resources – but even more, there are poverty, and inequalities. If poverty is a problem *per se*, rising inequality slackens poverty reduction, provides fuel for social unrest and polarisation, and can lead to the social exclusion of some (or many) citizens from the democratic process. Ultimately, inequality threatens the social fabric of a nation, just as inequitable economic growth can undermine the very sustainability of growth.

For India, the persistence of internal inequalities and regional disparities represents a serious hurdle in its rise to global power status. What is worse is that, notwithstanding relatively stable and encouraging growth rates, regional disparities in India are growing, too. To be sure, like for other young nations and emerging countries, the need to reduce domestic disparities has been a key challenge in India's nation-building process and development path since the very beginning. More than other countries, though, India must accommodate an amount of territorial, linguistic, ethnic, religious, cultural, social and economic differences that has no comparison elsewhere in the world. Not by chance, "Unity in diversity" is the expression that the founding fathers of Independent India chose as the motto that would guide and show the direction of India's development path as a democratic nation. Also, "*Sabka Saath, Sabka Vikas*" – Together with all, Progress for all – has been Modi's motto since he stormed to victory in the 2014 general election, and then again in May 2019. The votes of India's poorest states and most excluded citizens were decisive for Modi and the BJP's unprecedented electoral success, and for the new government this should be one more reason to focus on reducing regional disparities.

Much of India's nation-building process was precisely about holding and keeping together an extremely diverse country. In seventy years of history, notwithstanding all the hardships

– partition, religious and ethnic violence, secessionist movements, domestic terrorism – India managed to stay united, and to remain a strong democratic nation. But today the challenge persists: inequalities and regional disparities are on the rise, and if India really wants to become a regional power, much of its focus over the coming years must be on reducing these internal disparities, probably the most serious stumbling block on India's path to global power status. Moreover – as happened in the past – regional disparities may sooner or later pose a challenge to India's system of democratic federalism in a best-case scenario, and a serious threat to India's unity and stability as a democratic nation in the worst-case scenario, also by boosting centrifugal forces that indeed continue to exist in India[59].

The more global India wants to be, the more its governments must commit to reducing the imbalances and disparities that are keeping India and its people under the yoke of underdevelopment. "True democracy", as the Indian sociologist Dipankar Gupta once put it, "pays attention to social development and not just to sectoral growth"[60]. Indeed, high levels of inequality – including between men and women, and rural and urban citizens – threaten to subvert democracy and rob India of its

---

[59] M. Vaishnav and J. Hintson "Lok Sabha Elections 2019: A New Challenge for Federalism", *The Hindustan Times*, 13 March 2019. Rightly, the authors point out that "for over seven decades, India's system of democratic federalism has been credited with holding the country together amid unparalleled ethnic, linguistic, and religious diversity. India's post-independence constitution granted its sub-national states significant powers over many aspects of day-to-day governance. Shortly thereafter, in the mid-1950s, Indian states were reorganised on linguistic grounds, a farsighted political decision that defused many potential battles around linguistic identity. If federalism is the glue that has kept the world's largest democracy together, there are growing signs that this adhesive is becoming unstuck. The primary culprit is not relations between the Centre and the states, but disparities among the states themselves. For instance, the wealth gap between India's states has exploded in recent decades; research by Praveen Chakravarty and Vivek Dehejia demonstrated that, as of 2017, India's three richest states were three times richer than its three poorest states. Population growth has also been highly skewed".

[60] See D. Gupta (2010), p. 8.

human potential, whereas the commitment to improving living standards and the rights of all citizens should be at the foundation of any democratic republic, including the Indian.

Inequality, however, is not inevitable, and it seems that Indian policymakers are increasingly aware of the need to tackle this problem as a matter of urgency. Modi's first government implemented some important reforms that head in this direction, and has increased investment in vital areas such as infrastructure. After the 2019 election, though, Modi will have the strongest mandate an Indian Prime Minister has ever had in recent decades. This will allow him to implement even bolder reforms. Whether these reforms will include a serious commitment to redistribute wealth, increase social spending and its quality (above all in education, health and social services), attract investment to boost infrastructure, ensure financial inclusion, and enact legislation to provide access to the basic entitlements of citizens, is probably what most Indian voters were hoping for as they headed to the polls in Spring 2019.

5. A "Paper Tiger"?
What India Wants to Be(come)

Abhijit Iyer-Mitra

While India continues to sign multi-billion dollar agreements with arms vendors as antagonistic towards each other as Russia and the United States, the question one keeps hearing is what exactly is the endgame of India's defence procurement policy. This chapter argues that India is confused about both its environment and the evolution of modern military technology, to the point that it not only does not know what it is doing, but also that such confusion has many sources, mostly human. This starts from an unclear perception of whom to counter, confused political directives, and a lack of knowledge of the advantages of XXI century technology, springing from inadequate interaction with western militaries as well as a woefully misguided and out of date view of the defense industrial ecosystem.

To do this the chapter will first assess the threats that India faces as the author sees it. This regional threat survey will then be brought together into thematically exploring several security dilemmas that India faces. Separately it will list the major purchases India has made and the assess why these acquisitions are problematic. This will be done using a single major case study in land sea and air acquisitions. Finally it will move onto the human issues that affect military acquisition, including the lack of political direction.

Geographic Threat Survey

Pakistan

Perhaps the single biggest tactical threat India faces today comes from Pakistan. While India would rather see itself as a direct competitor to China (and indeed the rest of the world, would arguably, also prefer to see India as a competitor to China), India's failure to industrialise despite four attempts (under Nehru, Rajiv Gandhi, Narasimha Rao and Atal Behari Vajpayee)[1] means that the total power differential between the two countries is enormous. On the other hand, though the power differential between Pakistan and India is similarly massive, Pakistan has found ways to bog down India and equalise the differential[2].

The primary tool of equalisation involves the use of sub-state actors, a polite term for terrorists to bog down a large part of India's security apparatus in counter terrorism operations. This has four clear effects. The first is that it prevents a large portion of Indian ground forces on focusing on large scale state to state warfare[3]. The second is that internal security operations consume much of the security budget. Third, cumulatively points 1 and 2 mean that Indian forces lack both money and time to move from old style ground control and hold battles to newer paradigms of offensive war such as pioneering examples used by the French in Mali[4]. Fourth and finally, the lack of clear standard operating procedures and the consequent grey line that Indian troops have to tread legally in pursuit of counter-terrorism

---

[1] A. Singh, "The State and Industrialization in India: Successes and Failures and the Lessons for the Future", in *The Role of the State in Economic Change*, Clarendon Press, 1995.

[2] R. Jervis, "Kargil, deterrence and international relations theory", in *Asymmetric Warfare in South Asia*, pp. 377-397, Cambridge University Press, 2009.

[3] G. Kanwal, "Managing Internal Security: Case for a New National-Level Counter-Insurgency Force", *CLAWS Journal*, Winter 2007, pp. 91-101.

[4] M. Shurkin, *France's War in Mali: Lessons for an Expeditionary Army*, RAND Corporation, 2014.

inflicts a deeply corrosive, psychological and institutional psyche, where troops second guess their actions and are prone to being compromised given they can be made scapegoats of in the face of a highly erratic and unpredictable legal system.

Additionally the ongoing India-Pakistan faceoff over the Siachen glacier means that massive sums are diverted by India to hold the commanding heights at extreme altitudes and temperatures.[5] Cumulatively terrorism and Siachen then inflict significant attrition and fatigue on Indian ground forces. While mental health issues remain taboo in India, a high rate of "fragging" can be seen as an indicator of a problematic situation that goes merely beyond equipment[6].

At the equipment level however, the issues are different, where Pakistan instead of matching India tank for tank or plane for plane and ship for ship, uses a carefully crafted blend of nuclear blackmail and asymmetricity[7]. That is to say it does not fall in the equivalence trap that the USSR did *vis-à-vis* the US. For example, despite India going in for a large fleet of heavy twin engine jets like the Sukhoi 30 and Rafale (plus the upcoming Advanced Medium Combat Aircraft), Pakistan has stuck to a core fleet of light single engine fighters like the F-16 and the JF-17. Similarly, Pakistan pioneered the use of submarines in the South Asia theatre to ward off the threat of Indian aircraft carriers and offsets India's superiority in tanks with a massive arsenal of shoulder fired anti-tank weapons[8]. All of this is neatly coupled with an amorphous "damage threshold" which is to say, Pakistan will resort to nuclear first use, if it decides an alarming amount of its military equipment has been destroyed[9].

---

[5] "Avalanche buries 10 soldiers in Siachen", *The Hindu*, 3 February 2016.

[6] "The stress is killing Army: Suicides, Fragging claim over 100 a year", *The Times of India*, 9 August 2017.

[7] C. Bluth, "India and Pakistan: a case of asymmetric nuclear deterrence", *Korean Journal of Defense Analysis*, vol. 22, no. 3, 2010, pp. 387-406.

[8] B.W.B. Ho, "The Aircraft Carrier in Indian Naval Doctrine", *Naval War College Review*, vol 71, no. 1, Winter, 2018.

[9] V. Narang, "Posturing for Peace? Pakistan's Nuclear Postures and South Asian Stability", *International Security*, vol. 34, no. 3, 2010, pp. 38-78.

114   *India's Global Challenge*

This clever strategy means whatever advantages that may accrue to India from prolonging a war, diminish rapidly as India can never accurately calculate how much damage will trigger a Pakistani nuclear response. The problem set for India vis-à-vis Pakistan then is: How to reduce the debilitating and daily burden of counter-terrorism on the one hand, and how to score a rapid and punishing conventional victory as a punitive measure without triggering Pakistani nuclear usage on the other hand.

China

The Chinese problem for India is altogether different and responses seem both staid and ineffective. On the one hand China's impressive industrialisation has created vast surplus wealth, much of which is being ploughing into military modernisation. This certainly creates a massive imbalance. For example, just one new Chinese ship of the Type 055 class has more vertical launch cells for missiles than the entire Indian Eastern Fleet[10]. On the other hand it would also seem that the West's technology denial regime in place since the 1989 Tiananmen Square massacre is exacting a heavy price, preventing China from truly modernising its military. For example, China still has to rely on metal aircraft engines with high failure rates and has been unable to successfully fabricate crystal blade engines.[11] This despite a massive programme of industrial espionage.[12] The reasons for China's inability to translate industrial espionage into tangible results stem from the nature of Information Age technology. During the mechanical age manufacturers produced 70% or more of the equipment themselves. Technology however has devolved into so many micro specialisation and the rate of replacement so high, that the cutting edge of technology

---

[10] F.-S. Gady, "China's New Type 055 Guided Missile Destroyer Begins Sea Trials", *The Diplomat*, 28 August 2018.
[11] J.T. Lovell, R. Farley, "China's Air Force Has One Big Problem It Can't Seem to Solve", *The National Interest*, October 2018.
[12] J. Page, "China Clones, Sells Russian Fighter Jets", *The Wall Street Journal*, 4 December 2010.

today is in fact the Micro and Small sectors. This means an equipment manufacturer seldom produces more than 30% of a final product themselves, relying on a vast chain of suppliers and sub-contractors instead. As such stolen technology packets would be virtually incomprehensible as one would have to understand where each packet fit into a vast jigsaw. It is probably for this reason that while Pakistan is happy to accept a Chinese manufactured fighter (The JF-17) it insists on an Italian radar and avionics and a Russian engine.

China it seems is still in an age where it is striving for kinetic improvements to its equipment whereas the West has moved onto under the skin electronic revolutions, each of which reduce the sensor to shoot time and situational awareness to massive advantages on the field. The clearest example of how this principle works is that Vietnamese defences were able to take a heavy toll on US fighters in the 1970s, but Iraqi forces were unable to inflict significant damage on US forces in the 1991 gulf war and the far better trained and capable Yugoslav forces, even less so in the 1998-99 Kosovo war. While this is not to imply monocausality, the gaps between the "Kinetic East" and the "Information West" can only increase from this perspective given China being stuck in a middle income trap.

The threat posed by china to India then is as follows:
1. A long border where China holds the higher ground. This is disadvantageous to India from a ground attack perspective, but the enormous complexity of logistics and aircraft operations on the Tibet plateau give Indian AirPower an advantage in this sector[13].
2. The diplomatic support to Pakistan's terror proxies and military and nuclear support to Pakistan to maintain Pakistan as a credible tactical threat forcing India to divert resources from China to Pakistan[14].

---

[13] S. Joshi, *The Dragon's Claws: Assessing China's PLAAF Today*, New Delhi, Vayu Aerospace, 2017.
[14] L. Curtis, "China's Military and Security Relationship with Pakistan", Testimony, U.S.-China Economic and Security Review Commission on 20 May

3. A significantly bigger military, but one which may be at the same or at an inferior technology level as India.

4. Slowly developing naval power projection capabilities that would seem to indicate an ability by the Chinese to seriously challenge Indian dominance of the Indian Ocean littoral.

5. A much deeper industrial and economic strength indicating China can afford to prolog hostilities for a significantly longer period.

To this India's responses have been ambiguous at best:

1. Despite an apparent air advantage where the Indo-Gangetic plains are much closer to the Himalayan border, and extremely favorable to air operations, India has chosen a ground based approach which is literally an "uphill task". This has taken the form of raising mountain divisions of dubious impact, but enormously expensive both in human and equipment terms[15]. On the other hand India seems to be ignoring the air advantage considerably[16].

2. To date, India has failed spectacularly in any form or way to defray the political, diplomatic and military support that China provides to Pakistan. For example as recently as March 2019, India once again failed to have international Pakistan-based terrorist Masood Azhar, responsible for several attacks on Indian soil to be proscribed by the UN as a terrorist, primarily due to a Chinese veto[17]. Similarly India's lack of defence ex-

---

2009, The Heritage Foundation; T.V. Paul, "The Causes and Consequences of China-Pakistani Nuclear/Missile Collaboration", in *South Asia's Nuclear Security Dilemma: India, Pakistan, and China*, London, Routledge, 2005.

[15] S. Dutta, "Indian Army puts Mountain Strike Corps aimed at China in cold storage", *The Print*, 12 July 2018.

[16] R. Menon, "A Mountain Strike Corps is not the only option", *The Hindu*, 29 July 2013.

[17] V. Kaura, "India's Counter-Terrorism Diplomacy Towards China: Issues and Trends", *IUP Journal of International Relations*, vol. 13, no. 1, January 2019, pp.

ports (or indeed commercially viable defence products) means that India has failed to create leverage against China to equate Chinese sales of military equipment to Pakistan with Indian sales of weapons to Chinese near-adversaries such as Taiwan or Vietnam. And at a strategic level, India's misguided deference to Chinese sensitivities means that significant Taiwanese intelligence on China, remains ignored and unexploited.

3. While China brings both quantity and (seemingly) quality (caveated above) into play, India seems to lag behind in both. At the heavy end India's vast Sukhoi fleet suffers from wide-ranging problems at 50% availability or less[18] and much of India's single engine fleet is rapidly aging (such as the MiG21) or lacking in numbers (such as the Mirage 2000 & Rafale) or simply utterly ineffective (as the Jaguar fleet was during the Kargil war). Moreover current plans indicate that a logistical nightmare of having 7 different fighters (MiG 21, MiG 27, MiG 29, Mirage 2000, Rafale, Jaguar, Tejas) will continue with replacement plans envisaging a fleet of 7 different fighters (MiG 29, Su 30, Mirage 2000, Rafale, Tejas, AMCA, and the yet to be decided winner of the MMRCA contest). On the one hand as can clearly be seen there is a preference for twin engine aircraft with the attendant logistical costs. Logistically this represents a set of aircraft that fire 7 different air to air missiles, a significantly greater number of ground to ground munitions, 7 totally different engine families. Operationally, this takes a heavy toll on interoperability as due to operational security reasons of the supplier state, source codes that would allow Russian fighters to "talk to" and share data with western fighters will simply not be available. This means meager resources

---

44-58.

[18] M. Pubby, "Government admits only 55% of fighter aircraft fleet operational owing to technical issues", *The Economic Times*, 14 July 2018.

are squandered on many fleets of aircraft, without any synergy between the fleets, where quantity cannot be achieved, and quality is squandered due to the lack of interoperability. Similarly at sea, just one of China's new generation destroyers, the Type 55 DDG has more vertical launch tubes for missiles than the Indian eastern fleet combined[19]. Moreover India's destroyers combining as they do western and Russian equipment, suffer from the same interoperability problems ascribed to the Air Force earlier. Overall, India has neither a quantitative answer nor a qualitative answer to China, leave alone any means of negating china's vast industrial (and hence logistical and equipment replacement) depth.

4. If China has the resources to build up both a fleet of nuclear submarines and aircraft carriers to sail into and take on the Indian Navy in its own waters (or at any rate break a blockade of the crucial sea lanes of communication) then India's response has fallen into the classic Soviet trap of equivalence instead of opting for asymmetric approaches more suitable to India's defence budget and its industrial strength. For example, given the Chinese naval buildup two facts stare India in the face. The first is a tight budget and the second access to western technology that is arguably vastly superior to China. Yet instead of opting for a cost effective sea denial posture based on access to Western submarines, ships, electronics and acoustic databanks built up over decades, India chooses a sea control strategy, based around 3 different aircraft carriers each of which will carry a different aircraft[20]. The first of these, the Vikramaditya is a former soviet helicopter carrier flying the MiG 29K,

---

[19] One type 55 destroyer has 112 vertical launch cells, while the 5 *Rajput*-class destroyers that make up a bulk of the Eastern surface fleet have a mere 40 between all five.

[20] B.W.B. Ho (2018).

a plane that has had severe problems in Indian service[21]. This is to be followed by India's first indigenous aircraft carrier the LAC1, which will mount the domestic fighter, Tejas. This will be followed by LAC2 which will be built around the US electromagnetic catapult (EMALS) capable of mounting heavier aircraft and will carry as third as yet undetermined fighter. This un-cohesive fleet of Indian, Russian and Western fighters and ships will be further complicated by their escorts, the destroyers. India has been building a series of destroyers deploying a combination of Israeli radars and anti-aircraft missiles (the MF-STAR Barak 8 combination) that do not talk to the primary anti-ship missile on board the same ship of Russian origin (the Brahmos). Similarly, the anti-submarine fleet consists of US P8 patrol aircraft that do not data link with the Russian supplied anti-submarine helicopter fleet of Kamov 32s. In addition a split fleet of German (Type 1500) French (Scorpene) and Russian (Kilo) submarines, means the Western submarines do not talk to the Russian ones. In effect, India has a cacophonous mix of aircraft, aircraft carriers, missiles, submarines and submarine hunters, none of which fully talk to each other and exploit Western technological superiority, yet carry the hefty price tag that western technology commands. In other words, India neither has the quantitative superiority to challenge Chinese projection, nor do its quality purchases translate into operational quality on the sea due to severe inconsistency of equipment and the lack of deep data linking. Moreover the obsession with sea control means that a far more cost effective sea denial strategy has also been eschewed[22].

---

[21] G. Allison, "Indian Carrier Aircraft 'Riddled with Problems'", *UK Defence Journal*, last modified 4 July 2017.

[22] A. Iyer Mitra, "The Problem with India's Naval Build-up", *Mint*, 15 March 2017.

5. This cacophony of equipment, procured from suppliers deeply antagonistic to each other and politically opposed to allowing interoperability, has led to a situation of multiple logistical chains and meagre resources spread over various platforms. In short despite procuring vastly superior (to China) equipment from the west, the systems themselves do not confer qualitative superiority to India as they are pieces in a system of systems that require all the pieces to talk to each other. This is compounded by the multiple logistical chains which means that India's logistical budget cannot build a sufficient war reserve of just one type to offset Chinese industrial depth. In short despite access to superior technology, bad Indian procurement strategies mean the technological advantage is non-existent and the massive Chinese military-industrial complex will gain a significant quantitative advantage, and also possibly a technological advantage given the fractionalised and non-compatible Indian fleet.

To sum up, China poses a clear long-term threat to India. In spite of this, India has no clear strategy to deal with China, and has at every step chosen a high cost and unsustainable option dealing with China, be it diplomatically ignoring possible allies, going in for a disadvantageous ground centric approach, and an air and naval approach that seem to achieve nothing.

Terrorism

Terrorism in India can roughly be divided into 3 major categories: Islamist Terror, mostly but not restricted to Kashmir, funded by Pakistan; various terrorist groups in Northeast India, variously supported by Bangladesh and China; and finally Left Wing terrorism (Naxalism) that is largely indigenous. Of these terrorism in Kashmir has been the most prominent with the potential of destabilising the region the most as has been seen in iterations from 1947-1948, 1965, 1998, 2001, and yet again in 2019. However terrorism in the North East has been just as intense albeit with fewer international implications and with varying support from outside. Possibly the least discussed and yet most severe form was naxalite terror which at one point in its heyday controlled almost 1/3rd of Indias territory including large swathes of central, eastern and southern India[23].

Each of these internal security theatres have seen the use of force differently. Kashmir and the Northeast for example have frequently seen army deployments, while the Naxalite problem has been dealt with paramilitary forces. What is however common to all three and different from India's external problems is that India's responses to each of these has been ad-how and lacking consistency. For example, the fights against Naxals, for a while involved the slow but steady penetration of infested areas by the state. However when the Naxal expansion stopped and they were deemed to be a lesser threat, consistent efforts to defeat the problem simply petered out[24]. Similarly in Kashmir, despite repeated use of civilians as human shields by terrorists, mostly in the form of stone pelters, India is yet to come up with an effective Publicity or Operations strategy to defeat both tactic and its psychological effects[25]. Moreover knowledge gained during brief spells of success, have been allowed to lapse without follow up and have not been transmitted to following troop rotations. This has resulted in repeat cycles of violence with each lesson having to be re-learned on a periodic basis.

What this draws into focus is the ongoing inability of the Indian state, to collect, archive, institutionalise and on demand, retrieve learnings from past experiences. This means the same mistakes get repeated over and over again without

---

[23] R. Garge, *Security and Development: An Appraisal of the Red Corridor*, New Delhi, Vivekananda International Foundation, 2019.

[24] A. Sahni, "Fighting The Maoists With Mantras", *Outlook*, 25 July 2008.

[25] K. Shah, *Why Kashmir needs a new counterinsurgency strategy*, New Delhi, Observer Research Foundation, 2018; P. Bhatt, *Building effective counterterror narratives in Kashmir*, New Delhi, Observer Research Foundation, 2018.

the transmission of knowledge to successors and the attendant costs in life and material. This betrays an institutional problem that afflicts the entire Indian security establishment, but is most visible in internal security, due to the high publicity as well as frequency of operations and relative lack of secrecy.

Russia-China Axis

Perhaps the biggest fear in Delhi, since independence in 1947, and arguably a major concern of British India as well, was the possible emergence of a Russia – China axis. As a general rule, any alignment of these two great powers of Eurasia, was and continues to be seen as disastrous by India. For much of the 1950s and 1960s, India's main effort remained the breaking of the Sino-Soviet axis[26]. On one hand it involved giving China a leadership role in the comity of 3rd world countries breaking China away from playing second fiddle to the USSR in the communist world. At the same time it involved cosying up to the USSR at the cost of the US, providing important propaganda points to the USSR showing that the latter could be a reliable partner to non-aligned and democratic states. Indeed the plan worked quite well with Khrushchev and the USSR privately siding with India during the 1962 China-India war[27]. This support would become a major sore point, and one of the contributing factors to the Sino-Soviet split of the late 1960s. Indeed the policy was so successful that when Pakistan and India fought their third war in 1971, the USSR mobilised troops along its China border to keep Chinese troops bogged down in the north[28], to prevent any Chinese intervention in favor of Pakistan.

---

[26] J.W. Garver, "The Indian Factor in Recent Sino-Soviet Relations", *The China Quarterly*, vol. 125, 1991, pp. 55-85; "How Mao and Khrushchev fought over China-India border dispute", *South China Morning Post*, 5 August 2017.

[27] H.E. Salisbury, *The New Emperors: Mao and Deng : A Dual Biography*, New York, Harper Collins, 1993.

[28] K.G. Lieberthal, *Sino-Soviet Conflict in the 1970s: Its Evolution and Implications for the Strategic Triangle*, Santa Monica, RAND Corporation, 1978.

The situation in 2019 though is very different. Today it is China and not Russia that is the predominant power. In this respect, the worry in India is of a Russia that slowly but inevitably drifts into Chinese orbit. Indian fears in this regard can be enumerated as follows:

1. As Russia slowly but surely turns into an economy based on commodities export, China's vast markets, combined with Russia's alienation from the west and the west's search for clean non-fossil-fuel energy sources, will leave Russia facing a Chinese monopsony. This monopsony combined with vast Chinese infrastructural investments in Russia, will inevitably make Russia heavily dependent on China and hence subservient to Chinese imperatives[29].

2. The first of these imperatives, in the Indian mind is the collapse of Russia's Central Asian "backyard" or the stans, with their heavy dependence on Russia and energy wealth slowly being diverted towards China. If anything observers at the Shanghai Cooperation Organisation, have been reporting a slow but sure deference to China in these countries, with less than enthusiastic acquiescence by Russia[30].

3. The second imperative, that is truly terrifying to the Indian mind is complete land encirclement in Asia, with a China-Russia axis taking along Central Asia, Afghanistan and most importantly Pakistan in its fold. This would mean Pakistan would get its long cherished dream of "strategic depth" against India and India for its part would lose freedom of action in Afghanistan being denied a Central Asia base to carry on aid and

---

[29] *China and Russia: Collaborators or Competitors?*, Council on Foreign Relations, 2018.

[30] P. Stronski, N. Ng, *Cooperation and Competition: Russia and China in Central Asia, the Russian Far East, and the Arctic*, Washington DC, Carnegie Endowment for International Peace, 2018.

assistance programmes in Afghanistan[31].

4. In hard military terms, an arguable assessment is that the Russians were and still remain significantly ahead of China in some spheres such as data links and a limited spectrum of cyber warfare, in influence operations, in missile and aircraft propulsion and space technology, to name but a few. The worry is that even though the infusion of Russian technology into Chinese military-industrial complex may represent only a marginal addition, it would be a significant boost in terms of quality versus a struggling India[32]. For example, Chinese engines are said to have mean periods between maintenance at an abysmal 80 to 100 hours while Russian engines anywhere between 200 to 300 hours, compared to a western engine that could easily last well over 1200 hours. Thus an improvement, even from 80 to 300 would change the quality paradigm in favor of China by a factor of 3 or more and significantly alter the availability rates of China's already vast Air Force.

There is much by way of allegorical evidence to suggest that India is buying Russian arms in spite of a disinterest and indeed under protest from the armed forces, and much of this has to do with wanting to keep Russia sated, giving Russias military industrial complex a valuable client and delaying or preventing Russia's slide into Chinese orbit[33]. However given the vast disparity in purchasing power between China and India, at best this should be seen as a temporary stop gap measure, but one that comes at a heavy price for India in terms of interoperability within India's armed forces, a cost far greater than the cost of purchase of Russian arms.

---

[31] M.S. Roy, "Pakistan's Strategies in Central Asia", *Strategic Analysis*, October 2006.
[32] J. Bronk, *Next Generation Combat Aircraft*, London, Royal United Services Institute, 2018, pp. 5-12.
[33] J. Singh, *The Indo-Russian Defence Partnership: A Framework for the 21st Century*, Institute of South Asian Studies, National University of Singapore, 2016.

Indian Ocean Region

The Indian Ocean Region (IOR) is emerging as one of the main areas of military contestation in India's defence planning. The problem set that faces India here is quite significant. The IOR accounts for much of the worlds trade passing through. It also is a region of extreme imbalance. Some of the world's richest economies (Qatar, Brunei, Singapore, Australia) line this region, but so do some of the world's poorest and unstable states (Somalia, Tanzania). This extraordinary imbalance means that the IOR is one of the hubs of piracy both in the east around the Malacca Straits as well as in the west off the Somali coast[34]. Additionally the region is a major ground of superpower contestation with the US 5th fleet based out of Qatar and several elements of its nuclear forces based out of Diego Garcia. China for its part is building what could be the kernel of full-fledged bases at Hambantota in Sri Lanka and Gwadar in Pakistan. The threat matrix therefore spans the entire gamut from low intensity high frequency piracy right up to conventional great power contestation between conventional navies in conditions considered to be very favorable for submarine warfare[35].

It is here that India's first seemingly coherent response to the rise of China[36] comes in the form of the Quadrilateral (or Quad for short) comprising India, Australia, Japan and the United States. While the US already has a significant presence here, easily the largest in terms of tonnage in the IOR, it would seem that the US is keen for India to take over many of the policing roles for this particular area[37]. From this angle, the Quad should

[34] J.D. Pena, "Maritime Crime in the Strait of Malacca: Balancing Regional and Extra-Regional Concerns", *Stanford Journal of International Relations*, vol. 10, no. 2, Spring 2009.

[35] J.S. Sidhu, R.A. Rogers, "China's Strategic Ambitions in the Indian Ocean Region, India's Anxiety and the United States' concerns", *Malaysian Journal of International Relations*, vol. 3, no. 1, 2015, pp. 75-104.

[36] Y. Ji, "China's Emerging Indo-Pacific Naval Strategy", *Asia Policy*, vol. 22, no. 1, 2016, pp. 11-19.

[37] J. Hornat, "The power triangle in the Indian Ocean: China, India and the

be seen as an attempt to seduce India into a western war fighting paradigm and get India off its nebulousness. Yet it would seem that the attempt has not gotten far. On the one hand the US CENTRIXS system that can be plugged into any non-NATO surface vessel to share complete domain awareness has not been allowed onto Indian ships[38]. Consequently data sharing is does through extremely limiting voice and text commands, reducing the operations at best to passing exercises. Diplomatically too India remains unswayed as in "Raisina 2018" the ruling BJP's Ram Madhav questioned the value of the US and West to India's foreign policy, in a forum that hours earlier had hosted the Chief Admirals of the Quad[39].

Indeed, it would seem India's defence procurement in terms of naval systems betrays this same confusion, opting for complex and unworkable fleet of incompatible Russian, Western and Indian systems.

Nuclear Triangle

One major complicating factor in India's strategic planning is the existence of two nuclear triangles that directly affect India and mostly remain outside India's control. The first of these is the direct impact of the Pakistan India China[40] triangle and the second more indirect but equally consequential one is the Russia, China, US triangle[41]. China's actions seem predominantly dic-

United States", *Cambridge Review of International Affairs*, vol. 29, no. 2, 2015, pp. 425-443.

[38] The CENTRIXS system is to be a part of the COMCASA agreement signed between India and the US in September 2018, but has yet to see any operationalisation.

[39] M. Mirchandani, *Contesting the dragon: India and ASEAN converge*, New Delhi, Observer Research Foundation, 2018.

[40] L. Dittmer, *South Asia's Nuclear Security Dilemma: India, Pakistan, and China*, London, Routledge, 2005.

[41] E. Heginbotham, *China's Evolving Nuclear Deterrent*, Santa Monica, RAND Corporation, 2017; C.L. Glaser, S. Fetter, "Should the United States Reject

tated by this second triangle and the state of equipment, forces and numbers deployed by Russia and the United States.

China believes it will never have the ability to carry out a "splendid" first strike completely decapitating either Russia or the US and hence chooses a nuclear No First Use (NFU) policy to turn necessity into virtue[42]. In its quest to keep its nuclear arsenal survivable and relevant to emergence of modern technology, including precise conventional counterforce targeting, China has embarked on a major revamp of its nuclear forces including a plethora of missiles both land and sea based[43]. India for its part having on previous occasions faced both Chinese and American conventional and nuclear threats, saw nuclear weapons as a means of ensuring freedom of action. The fact that America no longer counts as a a adversary means that India's single point focus has been to acquire sufficient range and numbers to target the Chinese eastern seaboard with the belief that what is good for China is also good for Pakistan. Yet in real life this has proven to be an erroneous assumption. Pakistan's acquisition of nuclear weapons across a range of uses, from battlefield nuclear weapons to large city busters, combined with clever Pakistani nuclear threats aimed at deterring conventional retaliation from India against terrorism attacks emanating from Pakistan have created a major dilemma for India[44]. This stems from the fact that India's initial nuclear rationale which was to gain space for conventional action free from nuclear blackmail (a lesson brought home by the 1971 war) seems to have been well and truly checkmated by Pakistan. For example after the 2001 attack on India's parliament, an intended

---

MAD? Damage Limitation and U.S. Nuclear Strategy toward China", *International Security*, vol. 41, no. 1, 2016, pp. 49-98.

[42] B. Li, T. Zhao (eds.), *Understanding Chinese Nuclear Thinking*, Washington DC, Carnegie Endowment for International Peace, 2016.

[43] J. Stokes, *China's Missile Program and U.S. Withdrawal from the Intermediate-Range Nuclear Forces (INF) Treaty*, Washington DC, U.S.-China Economic and Security Review Commission, 2019.

[44] G. Banerjee, *A New Equation of Pakistan's Nuclear Weaponisation*, New Delhi, Centre for Land Warfare Studies, 2017.

leadership decapitation that was planned in Pakistan, India's military, though fully mobilised was unable to take action[45]. This stemmed from the fact that India's doctrine and weapons were not intended to deal with a slow escalation. Being large countervalue weapons, they were intended to inflict "massive and unacceptable damage" but could not be used for bluff to cover conventional actions. Some authors argue then that based on statements by former prime minister Vajpayee, former national security adviser Menon and former strategic forces commander Nagal, that India has set in motion all the assets required to transition to battlefield nuclear use and counterforce nuclear strikes[46]. It is believed that this is done so that India could match Pakistan's escalation dominance step by step and in so doing raise the threshold for nuclear use much higher than Pakistan's currently stated nuclear red lines.

Thus in responding to a real nuclear threat from Pakistan, it seems China's encouragement of Pakistani sponsored terrorism, safe under a nuclear umbrella has once again succeeded in forcing India to dilute its strategic game plan aimed at china, and divert precious resources to deal with the immediate problem that is Pakistan. Unlike the badly thought out conventional ground, sea and air responses, this diversion of resources is in fact born entirely of necessity. This highlights that fact that Indian defence acquisition and choices are as much dictated by exigent circumstances as they are by clumsiness and political compulsions.

East - West Dilemma

A major problem when criticising India's seeming ambiguousness towards the East versus West choice, comes from tunnel vision of look at strategic issues purely through military lenses.

---

[45] S. Kalyanaraman, "Operation Parakram: An Indian exercise in coercive diplomacy", *Strategic Analysis*, vol. 26, no. 4, 2002, pp. 478-492.
[46] C. Clary, V. Narang, "India's Counterforce Temptations: Strategic Dilemmas, Doctrine, and Capabilities", *International Security*, vol. 43, no. 3, 2019, pp. 7-52.

Breaking the siloisation and look at human and economic factors, one realises that India's reasons for hedging are critical to its overall development.

At the time of independence, much of the surplus capital available for investment lay in the west, dispensed either directly or through Bretton-Woods institutions. The supply of such abundant capital and creation of surge war demand, meant that the German and Japanese economic miracles were made possible, where a highly trained, disciplined and educated population could be rapidly reindustrialised through both money and market demand[47]. China benefited from a similar phenomenon, its industrial revolution based almost entirely on supplying cheap consumer goods to a massive western market, using economies of scale to lower costs and create new markets in lower disposable income countries like India. The world however has changed much since the 1940s. Today the West has little by way of surplus capital to spare given its economic woes and its markets are saturated with new opportunities hard to find. All of this has led some economists to speculate that China is the last industrial power and conventional industrialisation after this is virtually impossible with India having missed the bus for good[48].

However the industrialisation of China and its vast trade surpluses have also created a massive pool of surplus capital. This is surplus capital that India desperately needs. To gauge this one only needs to look at two statistics – Education and Infrastructure. India is in the midst of a severe infrastructural stagnation where inadequate power and linkages means significant lost opportunities and additional costs. One report alone estimated that a rationalisation and reinvigoration of India's infrastructure in order to unleash its full growth potential would

[47] T. Iwami, "Japan's Experiences under the Bretton Woods System", *Japan in the International Financial System*, 1995, pp. 36-61, doi:10.1057/9780230372634_2.
[48] A. Szirmai, W. Naudé, and L. Alcorta, *Pathways to Industrialization in the Twenty-First Century: New Challenges and Emerging Paradigms*, New York, Oxford University Press, 2013.

require over US$4.5 trillion dollars[49]. This is money India does not have but China does, and yet India is hesitant to let china enter the infrastructure market.

Infrastructure by itself however does not create growth and prosperity. Factories require trained labour (in addition to a conducive investment climate) and as of now India's education system is woefully inadequate at even providing the basic education required to be a modern factory floor worker (not the mention enormously restrictive labour laws that frustrate any form of quality control). Each year 13 million youth pass out of the Indian schooling system, which means that to generate a basic factory floor workforce at the rate of US$1000 per student per year, for 12 years of education one needs US$156 billion per year. To make this workforce truly factory floor compliant one needs to invest in trade apprenticeships and technical training. 13 million students for 3 years of such technical training at the basic minimum of US$10,000 per year costs India US$390 billion a year. This means that for India to reach a rudimentary level of industrialisation even lower than China's is looking at an annual budget of US$546 billion per year. India's current official spending on education is US$8 billion plus an additional 8 billion spent privately[50]. Clearly then the very basics of spurring industrialisation are nonexistent. Compounding this is the fact that unlike pre industrial France of Britain that were not representational democracies, such investments could be made piecemeal ignoring large segments of society. In China a similar policy prioritising the eastern seaboard ensured that such investments could come slowly and sequentially. India therefore is in no position to absorb the technology of the West as things stand. The labour force is not well trained or educated even to

[49] "India needs $ 4.5 trillion by 2040 to develop Infra: Eco Survey", *The Economic Times*, 29 January 2018.

[50] C. Mallapur, "Budget 2019 Must Tackle Missed Skill Development Targets Even As Ministry's Funds Go Unutilised", *India Spend*, 29 January 2019; *Indian Express*, "Economic Survey: Government spending on education less than 3 per cent of GDP", 31 January 2018.

the rudimentary standards of Western technology absorption and the requisite quality control (a function of liberal labour laws) is also absent.

The only country with such enormous surplus capital and a lack of clear cost benefit analyses (as evidenced by the Belt and Road Initiative) is China, which seems more intent on creating a short-term industrial bubble for its infrastructure companies and does not seem to have put much thought into the long-term blowback[51]. This would also mean that India could slowly transition into the lower end of Chinese production as and when China transitions to higher value addition products.

In short, taking a macro view of human and economic dynamics, what the West can offer india can't absorb and cannot afford to absorb, and what China can offer comes at a heavy strategic price that India seems unwilling to pay. Consequently India is stuck vacillating between alternatives and has no clear strategic vision precisely because it is trapped in a set of unenviable choices. These dilemmas ultimately filter down to security policy and contribute to the inability to clearly articulate or define adversaries exacerbating the operational confusion that plagues Indian military purchases.

Russia the West and Indigenisation

The socio-economic aspect discussed in the previous section certainly points to a clear inability of India to sequentialise its national priority set. However it does produce an interesting dynamic in the sphere of defence production. India's low human capital means that it is much more likely to be able to indigenise and absorb Russian defence technology that is still based on the manufacturing revolution of much of the XX century rather than the far more sophisticated electronic revolution that is based on Western XXI century Information age paradigms.

---

[51] T. Greer, "One Belt, One Road, One Big Mistake", *Foreign Policy*, 6 December 2018.

This is to say the learning curve of Indian labour is much easier in absorbing relatively crude Russian technology, the capital outlay required much more affordable, and the Soviet big single manufacturer model more suited to an Indian industrial paradigm that discriminates against and disadvantages the micro and small sectors that form the backbone of the western technological revolution.

Indeed while large countries can seldom be seen as acting with unity of purpose controlled by a single large brain, it is tantalising to assume that much of India's haphazard arms purchases from Russia are due to the fact that said Russian technology is easier to absorb, rather than the assumption of cluelessness or clumsiness. For example, despite an agreement to co-produce the Israeli Barak 8 missile, India failed in its development deadlines and the final product is entirely Israeli developed[52]. On the other hand Russian coproduction programme have been far more successful. India has gained some tangible knowledge in producing fighters based on its manufacture of the Sukhoi 30 and has demonstrated clear value addition to the Brahmos missile programme, managing to take over the software writing achieving a respectable circular error probability and indigenise significantly despite failing to manufacture the rocket motor despite technology transfer[53].

This of course throws up two further dilemmas when considered in the context of the previous section. First how will India absorb Western high technology when its human capital baseline remains so low? For example in a factory floor visit to the Saab Gripen assembly line in Linkoping, it was learnt that a significant part of the reduced cost of the more advanced Gripen E over the previous Gripen C/D version was through innovation on the human front. A worker at said Saab factory is invested in heavily to the pint that not only does his/her job, but is also responsible for checking the work of the previous worker in the assembly line. This requires an extraordinary level

---

[52] "Israel tests Barak-8 missile co-developed with India", *Economic Times*, 14 July 2018.
[53] "BrahMos missile: Here is all you need to know", *Indian Express*, 23 November 2017.

of training and discipline something India is unable to do, and therefore despite the advertised "low cost of labour" the mistakes of said low cost labour end up costing more than paying and incentivising Swedish high cost labour. This is just one in a series of labour force problems that make India completely unable to absorb western technology as is.

Another problem alluded to earlier is how does a pre-industrial country like India absorb technology from advanced industrial states that themselves have to cooperate in a vast common market space and localise it into just one country. For example the "west" that is to say the G7 plus the EU, South Korea, Australia et.al that are linked into the western alliance form one large trading zone with relatively free exchange of technology and suppliers[54]. This "industrial west" has a population of just over 1 billion people and a per capita income averaging get around US$43,000 and a total GDP of over US$46 trillion. Yet India belief is can duplicate this incredibly diverse and complex ecosystem into a population of 1.2 billion with a paltry GDP of US$ 2.6 trillion and a per capita income of just US$1.900. Clearly this is a mismatch that no law of economics can solve because it indicates two zones that are fundamentally incompatible, unless India chooses to enter the "west" from lower end manufacturing, which it rejects due to having delusions of a highly trained workforce which as we have seen before is non-existent[55].

Adding to this is India's failed domestic defence development efforts. For the ease of the reader the author will condense this confusing set of public sector research undertakings into the Defence Research and Development Organisation. The DRDO as it is called, expends huge amounts of capital each year precious money that could have been used for procurement - on indigenous efforts, almost every single one of which have failed

---

[54] S.-F. Enea, S. Palașcă, and C. Țigănaș, "G7 Countries – Advocates of the Global Business Cycle", *Procedia Economics and Finance*, vol. 20, 2015, pp. 193-200.
[55] P. Mallya, "India Is Creating Millions Of High Skilled Jobs, But Its Education System Isn't Keeping Up", *Forbes*, 6 May 2018.

spectacularly[56]. The reasons for said failure are not the subject of this paper, but needless to say the socio-economic issues discussed above, contribute heavily to the fact that the DRDO keeps failing and doesn't understand why it keeps failing, simply because it thinks in a security silo completely divorced from the reality of India[57]. The problem however isn't just of the DRDO failing but of the disproportionate opportunity costs its development efforts impose on the military[58].

For example, it has been trying to develop a light MiG-21 replacement since the 1980s and 39 years later, its initial design is still at the technology demonstrator phase[59]. In this period several western fighters such as the Mirage 2000 and F16 that were to be analogous to this light fighter – the Tejas, have gone through their development cycle and ended their production run. However, it was precisely because of the Tejas programme that India neglected a light fighter replacement with the net result that squadron numbers have depleted alarmingly and India simply cannot afford an outright bulk purchase for rapid replenishment anymore[60].

All of this points to one of two things. The first is that India's decision making is so siloised that it does not take economic reality into consideration. The second far more disturbing conclusion is that India's decision making cycles are hopelessly corroded by bad information inputs resulting in atrocious decision making. In the authors opinion it is probably the second option that is more likely as hard statistics and data are virtually impossible to come by in India and remain the perennial gripe of seasoned India watchers

---

[56] "DRDO Needs a Major Overhaul: House Panel", *Deccan Herald*, 24 May 2018.
[57] A. Gupta, "India Must Look Beyond DRDO for Defence Modernisation", *Quartz*, 16 August 2018.
[58] "India Spends a Fortune on Defence and Gets Poor Value for Money", *The Economist*, 28 March 2018.
[59] M. Pubby, "Tejas Light Combat Aircraft: The not so Indian fighter", *Economic Times*, 14 July 2018.
[60] V. Raghuvanshi, "India's New Defense Budget Falls Way Short for Modernization Plans", *Defense News*, 5 February 2019.

Land Sea or Air Dilemma

One extrapolation that can be made from the above narrative is that India's geo-political situation does not align with the East, but its economic situation is incompatible with the West. The denial of this reality for over 3 decades now means that the negatives (such as the light fighter replacement discussed above) have snowballed into a major issue that are too big to be fixed[61], and a holistic rectification of the situation is also not on the cards as there simply is no money for it as discussed in the education section above. In such a situation it becomes imperative for India to start looking at situations tactically and simply filling the blanks. To do this it will have to decide which single domain Land, Air or Sea it should chose to be superior to its adversaries in allowing the other to domains to remain as place holders. While there is no sign of Indias economic or security managers waking up to this reality, should they wake up, the hypothetical problems they may face are worth discussing.

Perhaps the least viable option is the ground dominance option. This is due to the extraordinary financial burden of maintaining a large army, whose physical presence is not enough to deter China and threatening enough to Pakistan that it will lower Pakistan's nuclear threshold[62]. In short the cost is not worth the results. As an example, ground dominance will not matter if the Chinese hold the heights on the Himalayas as every battle will literally be an uphill one that offsets indian ground force superiority[63]. Moreover Chinese air and sea superiority that results from an Indian ground centric focus will erode whatever short term gains the Indian army makes. Where this ground superiority will make a difference is in the Pakistan theatre, but

---

[61] R.P. Rajagopalan, "India's Big Defense Acquisition Challenge", *The Diplomat*, 22 December 2018.

[62] P. Chowdhury, "Right-sizing the Army", *The Statesman*, 16 October 2018.

[63] N. Bhushan, "The Mountain Strike Corps – An oxymoron in search of innovation", *Simply Decoded* (blog), 16 January 2016; A. Ahmed, "Decoding the Logic Behind the Shelving of India's Mountain Strike Corps", *The Wire*, 22 July 2018.

the sheer physical intimidation of an invasion force, entering and physically occupying Pakistani territory is more likely to trigger a nuclear response than the physically less threatening defeat of the Pakistan Air Force and Navy[64]. Moreover one has to consider given the educational issues discussed earlier, can a large corpus of troops be built up with sufficient cognitive abilities and freedom of action, given the low caliber of available manpower. In many ways this could work like the failed attempts in Vietnam in the 1970s Afghanistan through the 1980s and ongoing and the Iraq situation. The question is, if India is willing to bear the price of total devastation that say the Soviet Army faced against the Wehrmacht, or what Vietnam, Afghanistan and Iraq have suffered.

This takes us to the second option which is naval dominance, which is again a very costly affair. However the costs here are mostly capital costs and are much less manpower intensive. This enables India to overcome several of its human problems discussed earlier by islanding human capacity, choosing a small corpus of above average recruits, incentivising them and investing heavily in their training. The issue however is the time naval actions take to yield tangible results on the ground. For example, assume that India using a coherent western supplied navy, manages to devastate the Chinese fleet and block its sea lanes of communication and disrupt fuel supply and power generation on the Chinese eastern seaboard, will it still be enough to force a halt to Chinese air and ground victories in the Himalayan theatre, given China's massive strategic depth and reserves of fuel and other essentials? In all probability not, which means that while a sustained blockade may yield results, the tactical short-term consequences may be too devastating for India to bear, in much the same way as Athenian naval dominance was unable to save it from Sparta in the Peleponesian war and the same fate befell Carthage in the Punic wars. The three outliers

[64] M. Ahmed, *Pakistan's Tactical Nuclear Weapons and Their Impact on Stability*, Washington DC, Carnegie Endowment for International Peace, 2016.

to this principle have been Japan (till it faced America in world war 2), the United Kingdom, and the United States of America. The reason it worked for these three countries is because they are all either islands with a convenient moat insulating them from land and air actions and in the case of America it had achieved absolute continental dominance in accordance with the Monroe Doctrine by the 1900s, turning the Atlantic and Pacific into *de facto* moats.

This means what India needs is a force that is tactically decisive in a short span of time. That is to say an air force which as the Italian savant of air warfare Giulio Douhet put it "can destroy not just the eagle but also the eagles nest", which also conveniently requires low manpower that can be highly selective in recruitment and invest heavily in training and human value addition. For starters it solves the problems of Chinese quantitative superiority due to the fact that air operation on the Tibet plateau severely limit the effectiveness of China's air fleet[65]. Additionally, when dealing with ground operations, limited supply lines means that should India choose air centrism it can disrupt ground supplies and deal with a smaller localised Chinese army stationed in Tibet, negating any high ground advantage that it may have. Moreover the immense flexibility of modern air power means that on the Pakistan front, it can enact punitive measures in retaliation for terror strikes inside India without the physical threat of a large occupying force[66]. Airpower however bring some major limitations. India's supposed policy is to take parcels of land from Pakistan during a war to be used as bargaining chips for piece, and an air-centric approach may completely negate any possibility of such a peace, in much the same way that Israeli air dominance had to be coupled with occupied land in order to ensure peace with Egypt

---

[65] S. Joshi, *The Dragon's Claws: Assessing China's PLAAF Today*, New Delhi, Vayu Aerospace, 2017.

[66] D. Byman, J.G. McGinn, K. Crane, S.G. Jones, R. Lal, and I.O. Lesser, *Air Power as a Coercive Instrument*. Santa Monica, Rand Corporation, 1999.

and the Palestinians, with this approach failing with Syria[67].

Given the accumulation of educational, social, economic and military woes owing to decades of mismanagement and corrupted (or non collated and analysed) information and data, India will have to prioritise one of the three domains of kinetic warfare. Air power may seem the most suitable[68], but it remains to be seen if the vast institutional heft of the army will ever allow the focus to shift to an air centric paradigm of war.

Conclusion

The main problem that India faces today comes from the fact that it is a pre-industrial state, where much of policy making remains data free and prone to severe missteps given the lack of accountability and feedback loops. In interview after interview, senior government officials past and present complained of the fact that they had to remain ambiguous about Indian policy due to the fact that other departments of government were constantly facing failure. It would seem it is not some grand plan of strategic ambiguity, nor is it a sordid tale of strategic schizophrenia masquerading as ambiguity. The root of India's ambiguity is the fear that India is an enforcement deficit state that simply cannot deliver on its promises, and masks this inability through posturing and petulance. In short India's "strategic ambiguity" is quintessentially and institutionalised mechanism for failure compensation.

This lack of delivery produces a foreign policy that has to by definition be ambiguous[69]. The problem is this ambiguity then inflicts further damage on the security ecosystem as it has no

---

[67] K.M. Pollack, "Air Power in the Six-Day War", *The Journal of Strategic Studies*, vol. 28, no. 3, June 2005, pp. 471-503.

[68] C. Goulter, H. Pant, "Realignment and Indian Airpower Doctrine", *Journal of Indo-Pacific Affairs*, Fall 2018, pp. 21-44.

[69] S. Mitra and J. Schöttli, "The new Dynamics of Indian Foreign Policy and its Ambiguities", *Irish Studies in International Affairs*, vol. 18, no. 1, 2007, pp. 19-34. doi:10.3318/isia.2007.18.19.

clear political direction to work on and the constant failure of other aspects of India's governance such as education and economics affect the military in a way it can neither understand, nor process and compensate for.

This has led to an Indian military that is at cross purposes with itself, a military that cannot decide who to trust and whom not to as India's foreign policy will not allow it to make such clean choices. The choices it makes therefore are ad-hoc and fail to address India's security challenges holistically. This crippling inability to act then limits the options of the political leadership even further, forcing even more ambiguity on their part. Parallelly the magnitude of India's other problems means the resources available to solve those problems remains scarce and since the military of any country is the sum total of the human and industrial base of a country, all these other factors have a disproportionate knock on effect on the military.

This means India is and will in the foreseeable future remain a paper tiger and a marginal security player at best. It will not commit to any alliances fully, it will not prioritise one relationship set over the other, it will not prioritise one domain of warfare over the other. It will continue to buy incompatible arms from multiple sources and in the process only exacerbate interoperability issues within platforms, within service branches and within purported allies. The India story therefore it would seem is story of a successful marketing campaign, not matched by reality, and that reality is so bleak that no clear solutions seem visible on the horizon.

6. Facing Global China: India and the Belt and Road Initiative

Christian Wagner

India and China have a long and ambivalent relationship that has often been described in contradicting terms ranging from conflict and containment to competition and cooperation[1]. The Doklam incident in summer 2017 has underlined again that the unresolved border issue continues to be a constant source of bilateral tensions. China's close relations with Pakistan, the expansion of China's naval power in the Indian Ocean, and India's intensified both bi- and multilateral cooperation with Japan, the United States, and Australia in the context of the Quadrilateral Dialogue (Quad) are part of the mutual efforts of balancing and competition that both countries are pursuing in the wider Indo-Pacific region. However, it should not be over-looked that both countries have established new forms of co-operation in recent years. Economically, China is India's largest trading partner. Politically, both countries are members of the BRICS grouping (Brazil, Russia, India, China, South Africa) and the Shanghai Cooperation Organisation (SCO).

---

[1] T.V. Paul (ed.), *The China-India rivalry in the globalization era*, Washington, Georgetown University Press, 2018; C. Ogden, *China and India: Asia's emergent great powers*, Cambridge, Polity Press, 2017; J. Panda, *India-China Relations: Politics of Resources, Identity and Authority in a Multipolar World Order*, London-New York, Routledge, 2016; J.M. Smith, *Cold Peace: Sino-Indian rivalry in the twenty-first century*, Lanham, Lexington Books, 2014.

India is among the few countries in Asia that have refused to participate in the Belt and Road Initiative (BRI) from the beginning. India is also the only country that has justified its opposition against the BRI with the violation of its national sovereignty. The China-Pakistan Economic Corridor (CPEC), which is the flagship project of the BRI, runs through the Pakistan controlled part of Jammu and Kashmir that was claimed by India since the accession of the former princely state in October 1947. But Indian policymakers have also voiced their concerns over the rising debt of countries that joined the BRI and the lack of transparency of many BRI projects. There is a strong consensus in India in the opposition against the BRI[2]. Compared to this, there are only very few voices promoting at least a partial participation of India in the BRI[3].

India's relationship with the Belt and Road Initiative, however, is more complex and includes a variety of dilemmas and challenges on the national, regional, and global level. The argument is that even if India continues to reject this project, it may be slowly drawn into its networks, which are permeating neighbouring countries. The first part of the chapter tries to identify some of these dilemmas and challenges on the different levels; the second part will look at India's new strategies and initiatives that came up as a reaction to the BRI.

The National Level: Security *vs* Development

The Indian discourse on China is shaped by two diverging positions. On the one hand, China is India's largest bilateral trading partner; on the other hand, China is also seen as India's main

---

[2] T. Madan, *What India thinks about China's One Belt, One Road initiative (but doesn't explicitly say)*, Brookings, 14 March 2016; for an overview of the Indian debate see G. Sachdeva, "Indian Perceptions of the Chinese Belt and Road Initiative", *International Studies*, vol. 55, no. 4, 2018, pp. 285-296.

[3] See for instance S. Kulkarni, "It's time to reimagine South Asia: On India-China-Pakistan cooperation", *The Hindu*, 6 March 2018; T. Ahmad, "India Needs to Take a Fresh Look at the Belt and Road Initiative Proposal", *The Wire*, 2 July 2018.

strategic challenge. The most important controversial issue is the unresolved border question. India's humiliating defeat in the Border War of 1962 continues to shape the conversations in India's strategic community. The territorial conflict encompasses Indian demands for the Aksai Chin region in Kashmir whereas China claims the Indian state of Arunachal Pradesh as South Tibet. China regularly protests against the visits of high ranking Indian politicians to this region and has repeatedly denied visas to Indians from Arunachal Pradesh[4]. Moreover, the activities of the Dalai Lama in India pose an important bilateral security issue for China. Since his flight from Tibet in 1959, the Dalai Lama and large parts of the 150,000 strong Tibetan diaspora are staying in India.

After their rapprochement in the late 1980s, both sides set up a joint working group (JWG) on the border issue which has held 21 meetings until 2018[5]. Moreover, both sides signed various agreements in order to strengthen the status quo on the un-demarcated border. But border incursions like Doklam in 2017 have always marred the bilateral relationship. India viewed the construction of Chinese roads in this area as a strategic challenge to the Siliguri corridor, which is India's only land connection to its states in the Northeast. The crisis could be solved diplomatically and started off a new phase of collaboration after the informal Wuhan summit in April 2018.

Rapprochement since the early 1990s has also intensified the economic cooperation between the two Asian giants. Despite sporadic tensions and India's opposition to BRI, Chinese companies see India as an attractive market mainly because of its size and lower wages. So it is not astonishing that Chinese investment in India has increased over the years. In 2017, official Chinese investment reached nearly US$2 billion; a significant increase compared to 2016 with US$700 million[6].

---

[4] "China Denies Visa to Indian Badminton Team Manager From Arunachal", *The Wire*, 17 November 2016.

[5] Embassy of India, Beijing, China, http://indianembassybeijing.in/political-relation.php

[6] S. Dutt D'Cunha, "How China Is Positioning Itself Among India's Top 10

The real figures are probably even higher because those numbers only include investments from mainland China. But Chinese investment via Hong Kong, Macao, or via third countries like Singapore or Mauritius is not included in the official statistics. Moreover, investments that are generated from the profits of Chinese companies within India are also not included in the official data[7]. Therefore it is not astonishing to see estimates that Chinese companies have already invested more than US$8 billion in India up until 2017[8].

In recent years, Chinese companies have invested especially in India's growing start-up scene. Companies like Alibaba and Tencent have invested in Indian Online companies like Snapdeal and Paytm[9]. Chinese smartphone companies like Xiaomi, Huawei, and Oppo have set up manufacturing units in India and have increased their share in the fast-growing Indian market. India has also attracted Chinese investments in research and development. Huawei's Bengaluru centre is its largest R&D facility outside China and has recently announced the development of Artificial Intelligence (AI) capabilities in India[10].

Despite the Doklam incident, trade has reached more than US$80 billion in 2017 and has increased by more than 20% compared to the previous year. At the same time, there is a massive trade imbalance, and India has its largest trade deficit with China with more than US$51 billion in 2017[11]. India's exports are mainly raw materials; China's main exports to India are electric machinery. As part of their rapprochement after Doklam, in summer 2018, both countries agreed on tariff reductions

---

Investors Despite Bilateral Differences", *Forbes*, 1 May 2018.

[7] N. Banerjee, "China's Investment in India", *Millenium Post*, 26 February 2018.

[8] "China invested more than 8 billion USD in India until", *The Times of India*, 27 April 2018.

[9] S. Dutt D'Cunha (2018).

[10] "Huawei launches research and development centre in Bengaluru", *The Economic Times*, 5 February 2015.

[11] Embassy of India, Bilateral Trade, http://indianembassybeijing.in/economic-and-trade-relation.php (access 18 January 2019).

in order to promote economic collaboration. Moreover, both countries are in negotiations for the Regional Comprehensive Economic Partnership (RCEP). This free trade area will encompass 16 countries in the Asia-Pacific, which represent around 30% of global trade[12].

There seems to be an obvious complementary relationship between the BRI, a Sino-centric trade and transportation network with Chinese infrastructure investments on the one hand, and India's desire to attract financing and promote export-oriented manufacturing. The Modi government has initiated a large scale "Make in India" program in order to increase manufacturing by decreasing barriers to foreign investment among other measures. There were hopes that large scale manufacturing companies would relocate some of their production sites to India after the increase of wages in China. Hence India's dilemma on the national level is that its rejection of the BRI imposes large opportunity costs for its own development. The public discourse in India is more dominated by the "China threat" rather than by the "China opportunity". But this dilemma seems to be temporarily manageable because of India's high growth rates and its attractiveness to foreign direct investment.

The Regional Context: Changing Dynamics in South Asia

It would be mistaken to argue that India lost its influence in South Asia because of the BRI, which was officially launched in 2013. China had already invested in the region and had expanded its ties with India's neighbours long before 2013. These neighbours have always tried to play the China card much before the BRI in order to balance India's influence. India's neighbours have regarded China as an attractive partner because, when compared with India, it is politically neutral for them – i.e. they hardly have any major bilateral problems – and it

---

[12] D. Li and D. Kumar, *India-China trade barrier reductions*, HIS Markit, 13 July 2018.

has been economically more attractive[13]. This constellation has been supportive of China to enter South Asia. Hence, the BRI seems to have accelerated a process which was set in motion long before.

India is facing two different kinds of dilemmas regarding the BRI in South Asia: one linked to Kashmir, the other with its own efforts to promote connectivity in the region. First, the BRI may have the potential to also transform the relations between India and Pakistan and their lingering conflict over Kashmir. With the BRI, it appears that China has turned into a status quo power on the Kashmir issue, a position that is neither shared by India nor by Pakistan. Officially, China is not part of the Kashmir dispute. It is not mentioned in the resolution of the United Nations (UN) although it controls the Aksai Chin area of the former princely state which is claimed by India. But with its massive investment of US$60 billion in the CPEC, it is difficult to imagine that China, as a veto power in the UN Security Council, would have an interest in changing the present constellation in Kashmir. So, the Chinese investment in the region can also be seen as an affirmation of the status quo between India and Pakistan.

India's official position is that the whole princely state of Jammu and Kashmir acceded to the Union in October 1947. The presence of Pakistani troops in this area and the construction of roads and infrastructure by China, especially in Gilgit-Baltistan, are regarded as a breach of India's sovereignty. Already in 1963, India had protested against the Sino-Pakistan Frontier Agreement in which Pakistan provisionally ceded to China portions of Kashmir. Chinese investment in this region is not a new phenomenon. The Karakorum Highway (KKH) between China and Pakistan was already completed in the late 1970s. In order to make CPEC an economically viable project, it will be necessary to improve the KKH so that is can be used year-round.

[13] C. Wagner, "The Role of India and China in South Asia", *Strategic Analysis*, vol. 40, no. 4, July-August 2016, pp. 307-320.

However, India has also shown flexibility on Kashmir in its negotiations with Pakistan. In the negotiations with Pakistan during the composite dialogue after 2004, both sides reached an informal understanding in 2007 which would *de facto* have implied an acceptance of the territorial status quo by India. Although this solution was never made public, it was later confirmed by Pakistan's President Pervez Musharraf, his Foreign Minister Khurshid Kasuri, and the Indian Prime Minister Manmohan Singh[14].

China's status quo approach may also explain the proposals of the Chinese ambassador to India in 2017, when he declared that China could rename CPEC if India was willing to join the One Belt One Road initiative (OBOR)[15]. He also offered to "create an alternative corridor through Jammu & Kashmir, Nathu La Pass or Nepal to deal with India's concerns"[16]. But Prime Minister Modi has strengthened India's traditional position on Kashmir with his remarks on Independence Day 2016 on Gilgit-Baltistan. India's dilemma is that the BRI works in the direction of a status quo that is not shared by the present government of the BJP.

It is not without a certain irony that China's status quo approach in Kashmir is a much bigger challenge for Pakistan, Beijing's long-time ally. Pakistan is also facing at least two challenges. First, Pakistan official position on Kashmir argues that the whole territory of the former princely state of Jammu and Kashmir is a disputed territory according to the resolutions of the United Nations. Pakistan has used and triggered regional crises, like the Kargil War in 1999, to enforce an engagement of

---

[14] "Governments of Both Countries Now Have to Decide on a Time to Disclose Solution …", Interview with the Pakistani Foreign Secretary Khurshid Kasuri, *The Friday Times*, 1-7 June 2007, p. 6; "Pakistan and India Were Close to an Agreement", *The Daily Times*, 2 May 2009; "Musharraf: India, Pakistan Were Close to Agreement on 3 Issues", *The Hindu*, 18 July 2009.

[15] B. Kumar, "Chinese offer to rename CPEC if India joins OBOR could be in play again", *The Business Standard*, 24 November 2017.

[16] S. Dasgupta, "China hints it can rename CPEC if India joins OBOR initiative", *The Times of India*, 24 November 2017.

the international community in the conflict. China did not support Pakistan in the Kargil crisis. This raises the question of how far China would be willing to support similar strategies in the future, given the US$60 billion investment in CPEC that might be endangered by another military confrontation between India and Pakistan. Moreover, would China really have the interest to internationalise the dispute, like Pakistan wants, which may even lead to a referendum in which the Kashmiris may, for instance, opt with a probability of 50% to stay with India?

Second, the BRI has raised great hopes in all of Pakistan's provinces for better infrastructure and development. This has also increased the aspirations in Gilgit-Baltistan, a part of Kashmir that is administered by Pakistan, where there are growing demands for full provincial status in order to benefit from the BRI programs[17]. However, giving Gilgit-Baltistan the status of a full province would severely undermine Pakistan's long-standing position on Kashmir. If the region would become a full province, it will be difficult to uphold the demand that the whole area is a disputed territory. So reforms by Pakistani governments are always a tightrope walk, as they give more autonomy without granting full constitutional status. The new government of Prime Minister Imran Khan and his Pakistan Tehreek-e-Insaf (PTI) has introduced a large reform package for a provisional provincial status of Gilgit-Baltistan[18]. The major challenge for Pakistan will be how to achieve a *de facto* integration of the region into the Constitution without changing its de-jure status in order to avoid repercussions on the country's official Kashmir position. The BRI may, therefore, intentionally or not, contribute to an attenuation of Pakistan's position on Kashmir. This may diminish the risk of another Kargil-like crisis, which was directly undertaken by the Pakistan military.

Unfortunately, this constellation will not stop terrorist attacks from militant groups like Lashkar-e-Toiba (LeT) or

---

[17] A.A. Shigri, "A new status for GB", *Daw*, 24 October 2017.
[18] H. Malik, "Provisional province status proposed for G-B", *The Express Tribune*, 8 January 2019.

Jaish-e-Mohammed (JeM), which may have the potential to trigger another bilateral crisis between Pakistan and India such as in 2001-2002 after the failed attack on the Indian parliament. Pakistan's growing dependence from China may also make militant groups feel encouraged to continue or even expand their activities. Moreover, if CPEC will really strengthen Pakistan's economic development, this may lead to higher expenditure for the military. This may also fuel the arms race in the region in the long term.

Furthermore, India is facing another dilemma due to the Chinese investment in South Asia. It is often forgotten that Indian governments have also tried to increase connectivity in South Asia. Since the 1990s, India changed its policy towards South Asia emphasising with the Gujral doctrine the principle of non-reciprocity in conflicts with its neighbours. This marked a stark contrast with the Indira doctrine that led to various Indian interventions in South Asia in the 1970s and 1980s. Especially after 2004, the United Progressive Alliance (UPA) government of Prime Minister Manmohan Singh put a great emphasis on regional connectivity both bilaterally and in the context of the South Asian Association for Regional Cooperation (SAARC)[19]. India, however, lacked the great narrative on regional connectivity that is so successfully projected by China. Moreover, India's attempts have not been successful with regard to the promotion of intra-regional trade, which was still only about 6% in 2015, making South Asia the least economically integrated region[20].

India's opposition to the BRI has also hampered its own connectivity projects, with the Bangladesh, China, India, Myanmar (BCIM) corridor being the most prominent "victim". BCIM

---

[19] See Address by Prime Minister Dr. Manmohan Singh to the 14th SAARC Summit, 3 April 2007, https://www.mea.gov.in/Speeches-Statements. htm?dtl/1852/Address

[20] United Nations Economic and Social Commission for Asia and the Pacific (ESCAP), *Unlocking the Potential of Regional Economic Cooperation and Integration in South Asia. Potential, Challenges and the Way Forward*, 2017, p. 1.

developed from the Kunming Initiative which the four states started in the late 1990s in order to increase regional connectivity. In 2013, the Indian Prime Minister Manmohan Singh and the Chinese Prime minister Li Keqiang discussed the project during their bilateral meeting. After China integrated the BCIM into the BRI framework, however, India reduced its initiative in promoting the project[21].

Even though Chinese investments in South Asia might be simply extrapolated and even if only half of the investments will finally materialise, India will be encircled not only by a "String of Pearls" but by Chinese logistics, energy, and communication networks[22]. As India will continue its own efforts for trade and investment in the region, it cannot escape the BRI. It will be drawn most probably into the existing BRI networks in the neighbouring countries. This will become a challenge for Indian companies because the overwhelming Chinese investment may also shape the industrial norms and technological standards in the neighbouring countries in the mid- to long-term perspective.

Moreover, China has made it clear that the BRI is not an exclusive project but a complementary project that aims to integrate with other connectivity projects like the International North-South Transport Corridor (INSTC), which is promoted by Iran, India, and Russia[23]. The Iranian government, which has traditionally good relations with India, has already signalled its interest to include neighbouring countries like Pakistan in the

---

[21] S. Bagchi, "Beijing's Belt-Road plan overshadows BCIM meet", *The Hindu*, 23 April 2017.

[22] The "String of Pearls" refers to various port projects in Myanmar (Kyaukpyu), Sri Lanka (Hambantota), and Pakistan (Gwadar) which were modernised by China. There are concerns in India's strategic community that these ports may also be used militarily, In order to repay its loans Sri Lanka has to lease Hambantota for 99 years to China in 2017, see "Sri Lanka formally hands over Hambantota port on 99-year lease to China", *The Hindu*, 9 December 2017.

[23] "China calls for connection between Pakistan's Gwadar and Iran's Chabahar", *Pakistan Today*, 28 December 2017.

project[24]. Even if India refuses to link its connectivity projects with China, the neighbouring countries may do so. The division of Chinese and Indian connectivity projects may continue on paper, but it is difficult to imagine that these divisions will continue once the projects are implemented. It is more likely to see a slow but steady merging of Chinese and Indian projects in various parts of South Asia.

The Global Arena

On the global level, the different forms of collaboration between India and China overlay the controversial issues. For a long time, India has shown great interest in intensifying global cooperation with China. In the 1950s, India's Prime Minister Jawaharlal Nehru wanted closer ties with China in order to strengthen Asia's role in global politics. In his efforts to bring China back into the international system, in the 1950s Nehru even refused offers to make India a permanent member of the Security Council of the United Nations[25].

Since their rapprochement in the late 1980s, both states have intensified their global cooperation and have often shared a common position in global governance negotiations. Together with Brazil, Russia, and South Africa, they formed the BRICS group, which articulated the new self-confidence of the emerging powers. The BRICS have set up their own set of institutions – for instance, a think tank council and the New Development Bank (NDB), which was first headed by an Indian. China and India were part of the BASIC group which, together with Brazil and South Africa, committed to cooperate at international climate

---

[24] G. Sachdeva, "India and Pakistan can both benefit from Chahbahar", *The Hindustan Times*, 1 June 2016.

[25] A. Harder, "Not at the Cost of China: New Evidence Regarding US Proposals to Nehru for Joining the United Nations Security Council", *The Cold War International History Project*, Working Paper no. 76, Woodrow Wilson International Center for Scholars, Washington, March 2015.

conferences. In 2018, India (and Pakistan) became members of the Shanghai Cooperation Organisation (SCO), in which China and Russia are the most important players. India has also supported the creation of the China-led Asian Infrastructure Investment Bank (AIIB). With more than US$1.2 billion for various infrastructure projects, India became the largest borrower of the AIIB so far[26]. Because of China's dominant role in the AIIB, India cannot secure funds for infrastructure projects in Arunachal Pradesh, which is claimed by China (see above).

There are also at least two main controversial issues in the global arena between India and China. First, although China has agreed to the civilian nuclear agreement between the United States and India in 2008, Beijing is blocking India's entry into the Nuclear Supplier's Group (NSG)[27]. Secondly, China refuses to designate Masood Azhar, the head of the militant group Jaish-e-Mohammad (JeM), who is responsible for various attacks in India as a global terrorist, in the United Nations[28]. In both cases, China seems to protect the interests of Pakistan.

India's entry in the BRI could eventually also help to increase the bilateral cooperation in the global arena, but the BRI is a Chinese project, which is also perceived by the international community as such. The BRI is a "Chinese brand", in which there may be room for "win-win" constellations but not for equality between China and other partners. States that join the BRI are therefore perceived only as "junior partners" of China. This is in stark contrast to the perspective of Indian policymakers who see their country on par with China despite their economic and political differences. The perception that India would be regarded as a "junior partner" in the BRI is not acceptable for decision makers in New Delhi. Therefore, Beijing's

---

[26] R. Marandi, "China-led AIIB to spend $3.5bn with focus on India", *Nikkei Asian Review*, 25 June 2018.

[27] A. Aneja, "NSG still a far cry for India as China insists on NPT linkage", *The Hindu*, 15 November 2016.

[28] V. Singh, "China will review new inputs on Azhar", *The Hindu*, 27 October 2018.

efforts to woo India to join the BRI are likely to remain fruitless.

But India's opposition towards the BRI should not be mistaken as a general opposition to cooperation with China. On the contrary: at their informal Wuhan summit in April 2018, Prime Minister Modi and President Xi put their bilateral relations on a broader collaborative foundation after the stand-off in Doklam 2017[29]. One outcome was the agreement to cooperate jointly in Afghanistan in the training of diplomats[30]. Modi's speech at the Shangri-La dialogue in June 2018, where he made it clear that the Indo-Pacific is an inclusive concept that is not directed against other countries, was also a clear signal of rapprochement towards China[31]. So, India will not refuse closer cooperation with China, but only if there is no BRI stamp on the project. This means for China that joint projects with India have to be put under a different label, not BRI, which would give India the status of an equal partner.

India's Reaction: New Partners, New Formats

Facing China's growing presence in South Asia and the Indian Ocean Rim, India has reacted with a variety of policies. Of course, India has always had its own strategy for South Asia, the Indian Ocean, and Africa. However, China's massive engagement in these regions has caused many concerns in New Delhi. In August 2018, Foreign Secretary Vijay Keshav Gokhale declared before the standing committee in parliament, that "[t]he Strings of Pearls is real" and that India's "renewed stress

---

[29] H. Jacob, "Substance and optics of the summit", *The Hindu*, 20 April 2018; J. Malhotra, "From Wuhan to Buddha smiling in Delhi, a full week", *The Indian Express*, 30 April 2018; K. Bhattacherjee, "India, China should work together: Luo", *The Hindu*, 4 May 2018.
[30] "India, China launch joint training for Afghanistan, plan more projects", *The Express Tribune*, 15 October 2018.
[31] A. Aneja, "Modi's remarks in Singapore echo Wuhan spirit: China", *The Hindu*, 4 June 2018.

on connectivity projects was borne out of this perception"[32]. Hence, it is interesting to note that six months later Vijay Kumar Singh, Minister of State for External Affairs and former Army Chief, publicly rejected the concept of the "String of Pearls" in another conciliatory move towards China[33].

The most obvious reaction is that India will increase its efforts to promote its own connectivity projects. As already mentioned, India has a long tradition of supporting infrastructure projects both in South Asia and in Africa. India will focus its efforts on its own connectivity projects in the region, for instance, the Bangladesh, Bhutan, India, Nepal (BBIN) corridor, the Kaladan Multi-Modal Transit Transport Project with Myanmar, or the various bilateral projects like the ones in Afghanistan, the Chabahar port in Iran, or the railway system in Sri Lanka.

What is new is that India now seems to be more inclined to cooperate with external powers in third countries both in its neighbourhood and other regions. In South Asia, India has started cooperation with the United States in Afghanistan and with Japan in Sri Lanka. India and Japan have also agreed to establish the Asia-Africa Growth Corridor (AAGC), which will also cover the Indian Ocean[34]. Another example is the INSTC, in which India cooperates closely with Iran and Russia in order to get access to Central Asia.

The Modi government has also expanded its bilateral military cooperation in the Indian Ocean through new agreements with Oman, France, and the Seychelles. In the wider geo-strategic space, India has welcomed the revitalisation of the Quadrilateral Dialogue ("Quad") between the United States, Japan, and Australia. But India also seems to be deliberately reluctant to follow the American interpretation of the Indo-Pacific and to

---

[32] D. Mitra, "In Official Testimony to MPs, Government Revealed Full Story of Doklam", *The Wire*, 15 August 2018.

[33] "No encirclement by China, says V.K. Singh", *The Hindu*, 6 February 2019.

[34] J. Panda, "The Asia-Africa Growth Corridor: An India-Japan Arch in the Making?", Focus Asia, *Perspective & Analysis*, no. 21, August 2017.

upgrade the Quad format in a way that would signal a more controversial stance against China (see above)[35].

India has also shown a new interest in regional institutions like the Bay of Bengal Initiative for Multi-Sectoral Technical and Economic Cooperation (BIMSTEC) and the Indian Ocean Rim Association (IORA). This can only be partly linked to the BRI, but maybe India will appreciate the usefulness of stronger regional institutions that may also act as a counterweight against mostly bilateral instruments like the BRI.

India's more flexible foreign policy may also open up new opportunities to intensify the cooperation with the European Union. With its new Asia Connectivity Strategy, the EU has widened its foreign policy instruments in order to offer alternative connectivity projects with better conditions and more transparency than the BRI. This may foster EU-India cooperation not only in South Asia but also in the Indian Ocean and in parts of Africa.

Prospects: India's BRI Challenges

There is no reason to believe that India is going to change its position *vis-à-vis* the BRI, but this creates various dilemmas for India. Domestically, the non-participation creates opportunity costs. However, those may be easily compensated for as long as India has robust growth rates. The much bigger challenges are on the regional level. First, the BRI does not only cement roads in Pakistan and Gilgit-Baltistan but also a status quo on the Kashmir issue, which is not necessarily in India's interest. Moreover, the BRI could be regarded as an "external interference" in the conflict that has never been accepted by India. Second, India will continue its own efforts for better regional connectivity. But China will continue to invest on a much larger scale. Hence, future connectivity networks in South Asia

---

[35] S. Haidar and D. Peri, "Not time yet for Australia's inclusion in Malabar naval games", *The Hindu*, 22 January 2019.

– for instance in the telecom or power sector – may be defined by Chinese rather than by Indian standards. So, even if India continues to reject the BRI, it may be slowly pulled into it through its neighbourhood. On the global level, India joining BRI would give a boost to the bilateral collaboration. But as long as India will then only be perceived as a junior partner of China, it is difficult to imagine such a step.

There are no easy ways out of these different challenges and dilemmas for India. The first strategy would be to sit and wait. India is not in a position to enter into a competition with China on connectivity. During a parliamentary hearing on the Doklam crisis, former Foreign Secretary Subrahmanyam Jaishankar declared that it would be "suicidal for the Government of India to match port for port and airport for airport". "That would be a suicidal policy because it would be effectively entering into what is the equivalent 1970s arms race between the Soviet Union and the United States of America"[36]. His successor Vijay Keshav Gokhale conceded that China's financial conditions and the fast implementation of projects are attractive for many countries[37]. But after the initial euphoria about the BRI, there are more and more countries in which a critical reflection on the long-term repercussions of Chinese investments has set in, for instance in Sri Lanka, the Maldives, and Malaysia. This may open new avenues for India for its own connectivity efforts. Second, in order to be successful, India has then to be sure that its own and joint projects with partners like Japan or the EU have better conditions and offer higher transparency than the Chinese projects. This will also require more investment in the implementation capacity on the Indian side. Finally, India has signalled that it is not opposed to a closer collaboration with China in general. So another strategy may be to look for new formats to expand the bilateral cooperation with China under a different format.

---

[36] D. Mitra (2018).
[37] Ibid.

But even if India continues its opposition to the BRI, it will become more and more difficult for New Delhi to evade it in the mid- to long-term perspective. Chinese investment in India will continue, the BRI infrastructure networks in the neighbourhood may set up new norms and standards to which Indian companies have to comply. With its different dilemmas and challenges, the BRI will remain an interesting test case for India to see if the often quoted "Wuhan spirit"[38] has really marked the beginning of a new phase of cooperation or was just an interlude in the long-term strategic competition between the two Asian giants.

---

[38] A. Aneja, "Wuhan spirit should spur 'natural partner' India to join Belt and Road initiative: China", *The Hindu*, 27 August 2018.

7. India, Europe and Italy: Time to Boost Partnership

Claudio Maffioletti

India's geopolitical strategy and economic interests are defined by its historic partnerships with Japan, Iran, and Russia, along with its need to counterbalance China's extending areas of influence in Southeast Asia and Africa. At the same time, the diaspora of Indians in North America, the United Kingdom, the Gulf Countries, Singapore and Oceania has been acting for the past few generations as a formidable catalyst for generating trade flows and cross-border investments.

Today, as India has been recognised as both a dynamic demographic and economic power, it is also facing major challenges: the need to ensure jobs for an ever-growing young population; to increase its attractiveness for foreign investors; to boost its infrastructural network and manufacturing capacity, supported by the availability of skilled manpower; to bridge its increasing income, gender, and urban/rural divides; to propose a suitable solution to its urban development, able to effectively implement smart and sustainable measures.

Within this framework, does Europe still represent an opportunity to boost India's global ambitions? And against this backdrop, what role should Italy play? On the basis of the history of economic relationships between Italy and India, and on the areas and expertise Italy is renowned for in the world, what should an "Italian grand strategy" for India look like? And what actions could be taken into consideration to implement it?

India's Global Ambitions and Europe

From "look east" to "act east"

India's *Look East Policy* was shaped between 1991 and 2004, when the country's economic liberalisation began, along with moving away from the Cold-War era approach, in which India had relatively hesitant diplomatic relationships with Southeast Asia. Enacted during the governments of Prime Ministers P.V. Narasimha Rao (1991-1996) and Atal Bihari Vajpayee (1998-2004), it was continued by Prime Minister Manmohan Singh (2004-2014) and re-launched as *Act East* by Prime Minister Narendra Modi. This policy is an example of a bipartisan and successful attempt to define a leading role for India in the region, by shaping strategic and military cooperation with nations in Southeast Asia (Myanmar, Thailand, Philippines, Singapore, Vietnam and Cambodia) and the Pacific area (Japan, South Korea) concerned about the expansion of China's economic and strategic influence.

India's relationship with Japan is particularly well rooted and solid. As part of the recently launched concept of an "Indo-Pacific Region", the two countries have jointly initiated the "Asia-Africa Growth Corridor" infrastructure project aimed at economically connecting Africa and Southeast Asia through the Indian Ocean by developing power infrastructure, roads, railways and ports.

To counterbalance China's assertiveness in the region acquired through the Belt and Road Initiative (BRI), the guidelines of the *Act East Policy* were redefined in June 2018. They identify a pivotal area for the development of India's political and economic influence: a Free, Open, Inclusive Indo-Pacific (FOIIP) extending from the eastern "shores of Africa to the (western) shores of the Americas"[1]. As an alternative to China's

---

[1] Prime Minister Narendra Modi's speech during International Institute for Strategic Studies's annual Shangri-La dialogue in Singapore on June 1, 2018

BRI, within the context of the FOIIP, India proposes a series of investments for the infrastructural development of ports in Bangladesh, Sri Lanka, Iran, and Oman, and extension of bilateral agreements on maritime security.

The FOIIP introduces a few important changes to India's approach to international relations. It abandons its traditional bilateral approach to embrace a multilateral one, keeping the Association of Southeast Asian Nations (ASEAN) at the centre of a series of agreements with regional (Japan, Indonesia, Singapore) and non-regional (Australia, France, United States) countries. It fosters the promotion of an international rule-based order aimed at guaranteeing free maritime movements and security along with resolving disputes through international laws.

Another important element of India's neighbouring policy is the partnership with Iran: in February 2018, during Iran President Rouhani's visit to India (the first in 10 years), a lease agreement for the port of Chabhar was signed by India, Iran and Afghanistan to improve maritime connectivity. India has strong relationships with the United Arab Emirates, one of its main petrol suppliers.

Notwithstanding the historical geopolitical rivalry with China, which led to a brief yet bloody confrontation in 1962 for a border dispute in Jammu and Kashmir, and China's support of Pakistan, dialogue and interactions have been steady: visits by President Xi Jinping to Delhi and by Prime Minister Modi to Beijing have been frequent.

Indo-European relations: waiting for the FTA, focus on smart and sustainable cities

The diplomatic relations between India and the EU date back to 1962, and the 1994 EU-India Cooperation Agreement defines the legal framework of institutional relations between the two, together with regular summits that have strengthened the political and economic collaborations in specific sectors. In 2007, negotiations for a Free Trade Agreement (FTA) between the EU and India began; yet they came to a standstill, given the distance between the parties with regard to issues concerning barriers limiting market access to specific goods and services by EU companies, public tendering, regulations on investment protection and sustainable development. The EU-India FTA would have a tremendous effect for both economies. Considering that India unilaterally suspended most of the FTAs with other countries, this would give the EU a "first mover advantage". In addition, India recently communicated the forthcoming expiry of all the Bilateral Investment Treaties (BIT), including those with European countries, which will need to be re-negotiated at a communitarian level. Yet, it is unrealistic to imagine their ending in the short/mid-term.

In the meanwhile, since 2014, India has been upgraded to "Middle-Income Country" status, and is therefore no longer a recipient of funding from the EU for international cooperation and development.

In March 2016, the EU-India Agenda for Action – 2020 defined a common roadmap to strengthen this partnership. Within its framework, a strong focus was put on clean technologies, which have become one of the strong points of the EU's strategy towards India. The EU-India Clean Energy and Climate Partnership intends to promote

> access to and dissemination of clean energy and climate friendly technologies and encourages research and the development of innovative solutions. It guides the energy and climate policy dialogue between the EU and India and helps in supporting joint projects and joint research. Current areas of collaboration include activities in offshore wind energy, rooftop solar and solar parks, integration of renewable energy and storage, smart grids, biofuels and energy efficiency in buildings[2].

---

[2] *Joint Declaration Between The European Union And The Republic Of India On A Clean Energy And Climate Partnership*, The Republic of India and the European Union, and also *Eu-India Joint Statement On Clean Energy And Climate Change*, New Delhi, 6 October 2017.

On 10 December 2018, the EU announced its new strategy for India over the next 10-15 years: international security based on rule-of-law, sustainable development based on a circular economy; cross-border investments and innovation are its main pillars.

The new approach identifies the connectivity and mobility of people and goods in regard to infrastructural investments and development: since 2014, the EU has financed approximately €8 billion for bilateral connectivity in the region (ASEAN's Master Plan on Connectivity, ERASMUS+): the European Fund for Sustainable Development (EFSD), the Investment Facility for Central Asia and the Asia Investment Facility will play a pivotal role in directing public and private funding. From a trade perspective, the EU is co-financing (in coordination with the European Development Bank and as part of the Institutional Partnership framework) several interventions in the area of Smart Cities, sustainable urbanisation, renewable energy and actions aimed at reducing India's carbon footprint. With regard to support for and development of the private sector, over the 2014-2020 period, approximately €2 billion has been allocated, mainly directed to Sustainable Development Goals (SDGs) in India.

Considering that the UK has traditionally been the entry-way for Indian investments in the EU, with Brexit, how are EU nations positioning themselves towards the Indian market? Germany, France, Belgium and Italy are some of the most present and active countries in India.

Their total trade with India in the financial year 2018 amounted to approximately US$56 billion, 7.5% of total Indian trade and 56% of Europe's trade with India[3].

At the same time, with more than US$21.5 billion invested between 2013-2018, European companies top the list of investors in India[4], counting approximately 6000 companies

---

[3] Indian Ministry of Commerce, Export/Import Data Bank.
[4] Reserve Bank of India. The calculation does not consider Foreign direct Investments (FDIs) from routed flows through Mauritius, Singapore and other

established in the country that have generated direct and indirect employment for 6.2 million people[5].

Yet a strong limitation to an increased presence of European and Italian companies in the Indian market is represented by a series of barriers posed by the Indian regulatory framework: a steady increase of custom duties applied to specific product categories (steel products, leather goods, footwear, IT products), along with complex and costly procedures defined by the Bureau of Indian Standards for imports of products ranging from white goods to furniture and lighting, from plants and fruits to treated meats and cheeses, from steel products to electronic items.

In addition to this, it is necessary to obtain, often exclusively through a local partner, import licenses issued by different Indian authorities: the Food and Safety Standards Authority of India (FSSAI) for food items (which includes a prior and compulsory inspection and testing of samples); the Ministry of Health and Family Welfare for pharmaceutical items, cosmetics and medical devices; the Department of Telecommunications for wireless devices.

The Indian Context: Challenges and Opportunities

When it comes to defining a strategic approach and the specific actions to be implemented by European and Italian stakeholders, a number of factors characterising the Indian economic, political, social, and cultural context need to be considered. Whilst estimates indicate a GDP growth of 7.3% in 2018 and a forecast growth of 7.4% in 2019[6], India has improved its position in some international rankings: in 2017, it moved from the 55th to

---

tax havens.

[5]   https://cdn2-eeas.fpfis.tech.ec.europa.eu/cdn/farfuture/bKxeumPzOb-F8OEde6SrD5qWyKo9-suTMQp3ZZLfv93M/mtime:1542703624/sites/eeas/files/eu-india_factsheet_november_2018.pdf

[6] International Monetary Fund.

the 40th position in the Global Competitiveness Index (World Economic Forum); in 2018, it rose from the 100th to 77th position in the Ease of Doing Business Index (World Bank). Indian corporations' turnover has grown at an average of 30% each year (McKinsey Global Institute), the expenditure for goods and services of its ever-growing, urbanised and young middle class is constantly increasing, as 60% of India's GDP is generated by the domestic market; the implementation of an important tax reform, the Goods and Services Tax (GST), is ushering in a much-needed harmonisation of India's federal fiscal system, and a simplification of internal exchanges. There still remain several challenges and these will need to be addressed by the new NDA government elected in May 2019 elections. Europe and Italy have the opportunity to play an important role.

Manufacturing and skill development: the - shaking? - pillars of India's growth story

Information and Communication Technology (ICT) and Business Processes Outsourcing (BPO) for multinational and foreign corporations have been the powerhouse of Indian growth: 65% of the country's GDP comes from the services sector, followed by manufacturing (18%) and agriculture (17%). Yet the vast majority of India's workforce (approximately 60%) is still employed in the primary sector, whilst the manufacturing capacity of Indian industries is not able to satisfy ever-increasing domestic demand, resulting in a chronic trade balance deficit, with significant exposure towards India's threatening and giant neighbour, China. At the same time, only a mere 4.7% of India's workforce possess the skills required by the industry. These structural limitations have been one of the priorities of Prime Minister Modi's efforts: Make-in-India and Skill India were launched at the very beginning of his tenure, between 2014 and 2015. The target by 2022 is to increase the impact of manufacturing on India's GDP from the present 18% to 25% and India's export from US$300 billion to US$700 billion; train 250 million professionals, skilled labour and manpower.

Four years after these projects were launched, the results and achievements present a picture in chiaroscuro: Foreign Direct Investments are consistently increasing (from US$16 billion in 2014 to US$37 billion in 2018, with an average yearly increase of 26%), but investments in manufacturing in 2018 decreased 10% from 2017[7]. Conversely, the employability of skilled manpower grew from 40% in 2017 to 46% in 2018, but still remains way below market demand[8]. On top of this, the National Sample Survey Office (NSSO) has published the official unemployment rate, which stands at 6.1%, the highest since 1972-1973.

Physical and digital infrastructure, logistics, retail and e-commerce

India requires a total investment of US$780 billion by 2025 to meet its requirements for roads, highways, ports, airports, railways, metros and telecommunications network development, along with its needs for power generation, from both traditional and renewable sources, transmission and distribution.

- *Highways*: in 2018, the length of the existing network reached 122,000 km (it was 93,000 in 2014). In 2019, a further increase of 50,000 km is expected.
- *Airports*: in 2018 there were 102; the target by 2020 is to increase to 250 airports, with a specific focus on tier-II cities and an increased capacity from the current 350 million passengers to 550 million by 2030.
- *Railways and metros*: the government allocated US$23 billion to address issues of capacity, by doubling the 18,000 km of the existing network and widening to three and four lines. In 2018, 25 metro projects in 10 Indian cities were approved, for a total of 500 km of underground and surface lines.

---

[7] Reserve Bank of India, "Foreign Direct Investment Flows to India", *Annual Report 2018*, Appendix, Table 9.

[8] India Skill Report 2018.

- *Smart Cities*: launched in 2016 by the central government, the Smart Cities Mission made available approximately US$34 billion by 2023 to identify, select and implement greenfield and brownfield (retrofitting) projects in existing urban contexts. In 2018, 100 project proposals were approved, and 20 are presently under implementation[9].

Such an ambitious infrastructure development plan requires substantial investments, and a policy-making and project management framework able to define and implement a scalable and innovative approach, in line with the expectations of domestic and international private and institutional investors. The National Infrastructure Investment Fund (NIIF), in which the Indian government possesses a 49% stake, whilst the remaining 51% is in the hands of international and domestic investors, was established precisely to attract necessary investments.

Agriculture, farm mechanisation and food processing

With approximately 160 million hectares of agricultural land and more than 20 different agro-climatic zones, India possesses the second-largest amount of cultivable land worldwide. Yet 85% of this is comprised of small and micro agricultural land holdings, making it challenging for owners to invest in machinery and technology. Moreover, the government's response to the 2007-2008 spikes in global food prices continue to reverberate in India: subsidising agricultural industries and increasing domestic prices has led to the hoarding of food stocks and inflationary pressure, further accelerated by increasing consumer demand[10]. A suitable solution to India's spiralling food prices would be more and better infrastructure, as their inefficiencies

---

[9] Smart Cities Mission, http://smartcities.gov.in/content/innerpage/cities-profile-of-20-smart-cities.php
[10] International Monetary Fund, *Understanding India's Food Inflation: The Role of Demand and Supply Factors*, 2016.

hinder the growth of the sector by undercutting the shipment of produce to points of sale. As a consequence, only 40% of fresh produce is preserved, processed and distributed. On the innovation front, India should invest in upgrading its agricultural research labs, collaborate globally to import machinery and methods, and adopt modern irrigation and drainage systems. There has to be systemic change, if India is to embrace sustainable, highly productive and exportable agriculture[11].

These weaknesses afford several opportunities: there is a need to increase the productivity and variety of agricultural products; introduce technologies for cultivation and preservation (cold chain); increase sustainable and natural agriculture and food processing and improve skills in the fields of agronomy and mechanisation. Italy is one of India's main suppliers of technologies for farm mechanisation, post-harvesting, cold-chain, food processing and packaging, and is one of the leaders worldwide as far as agro-industry R&D is concerned. Italy is the right partner for supporting India in achieving the objectives established by the Indian government and investment plans for this sector (some US$160 billion).

Lastly, it is useful to point out the constant income growth of Indian households: according to the World Economic Forum[12], the expenditures of Indian families will increase from the current US$1.5 billion to US$6 billion in 2030. Interestingly, this growth will be driven by consumption in both mega and medium sized cities, which will make use of smart and online technologies. Even though limited by a retail sector still at a nascent stage and crippled by both exorbitant real estate prices in urban centres and insufficient logistic and distribution infrastructure, the Indian market's appeal for

[11] World Economic Forum, "Agricultural Reforms: Inefficiencies are hindering India's Agricultural Sector", https://toplink.weforum.org/knowledge/insight/a1Gb0000000LOoTEAW/explore/dimension/a1Gb00000015QdpEAE/summary
[12] World Economic Forum, *Future of Consumption in Fast-Growth Consumer Markets: India*, January 2019.

European and Italian exporters of consumer goods continues to be very high.

Cultural diversity and complexity

Whilst preparing a marketing strategy to approach the Indian market, a set of diverse cultural values and factors affecting Indian consumers' behaviour needs to be considered: as Rama Bijapurkar would put it,

> Indians belong to many centuries at the same time. A farmer who understands ecological balance and the power of the Internet coexists with a nuclear scientist who insists that he needs his son to light his funeral pyre, so that he is not trapped in yet another cycle of birth and death[13].

A secular state, granting the constitutional right to freedom of religion and to practise, preach, and propagate any religion, India features perhaps the widest cultural diversity worldwide within the borders of a single political entity. All the main religious groups are present: Hinduism (80% of the population), Islam (14%), Christianity (2%), Sikhism (2%), Buddhism (1%), and Jainism (0.5%)[14].

With 780 languages spoken within its territories, belonging to the Indo-Aryan, Iranian, Nuristani, Dravidian, Austro-Asiatic, and Sino-Tibetan families of languages, India also hosts formidable linguistic diversity. The Indian Constitution does not give any language the status of national language and only recognises 22 "scheduled languages". Two "contact languages" have played an important role in India's history: Persian, the court language during the Mughal Period, was used as the administrative language and then supplanted by English during the colonial era. As per the latest census in 2011, India has more than 500 million speakers of Hindi, 50 million speakers

---

[13] R. Bijapurkar, *We Are Like That Only. Understanding the Logic of Consumer India*, Penguin Books, 2009.
[14] 2011 Census.

of Urdu, 260,000 speakers of English, 97 million speakers of Bengali, 83 million speakers of Marathi and many, many others.

To complete this summary of India's diversity, the caste system: Article 15 of the Indian Constitution prohibits caste discrimination and Article 17 declared the practice of untouchability to be illegal. Yet societal stratification, and the inequality that comes with it, still exists in India. Government policies aim at reducing this inequality by reservation quotas for lower classes, but paradoxically have also created an incentive to keep this stratification alive.

Italy's Grand Strategy for India: Some Inputs

After India's internal market opened up to foreign investments, trade between the two countries greatly increased: from €700 million in 1991 to € 8.5 billion in 2011. Yet since 2012 a negative trend in total trade has been registered, touching its lowest point in 2014, with total trade of €7.2 billion. The reasons for this slowdown are many, yet there are two factors that seem to have played a major role.

The diplomatic tensions caused by the disagreement over the legal jurisdiction of the Enrica Lexie case, wherein two Italian marines aboard the Italian-flagged commercial oil tanker were alleged by Indian authorities to have killed two Indian fishermen and subsequently detained in India without formal charges, were used in both countries as an argument to ignite public opinion over domestic issues.

This, in turn, generated a widespread negative perception, especially on the Italian side, of India and Indian companies, which has undermined the attractiveness of the Indian market.

Moreover, Small and Medium Enterprises (SMEs), the economic backbone of both countries, find it difficult to identify and allocate the suitable financial and organisational resources needed to implement a long-term strategy and commitment to approach one another's markets. On the contrary, there are many cases of Indian and Italian SMEs adopting a short-sighted, hit-and-run approach in the hope of a quick win. Most often, this has resulted in failure and subsequent disappointment.

In addition, there is a lack of a coordinated and systemic approach by both public and private stakeholders and financial institutions (banks from both countries are present only through representative offices) able to jointly support and facilitate the entry and "soft landing" of Italian and Indian SMEs in each other's countries, possibly through pilot projects in specific sectors and areas.

At the same time, to counterbalance this trade standstill, the past five years have seen a steady integration of the two economies through cross-border investments in both countries. There are approximately 630 Italian companies that have invested in India (they were 450 in 2013), mainly concentrated in the manufacturing hubs in the northern regions (Delhi, Gurgaon, Noida), Maharashtra (Mumbai and Pune), Tamil Nadu (Chennai) and Karnataka (Bangalore). In the 2013-2018 period investments by Italian companies in India amounted to approximately US$1.3 billion, making Italy the 10th investor in the country. A mapping of the most important Italian investments in India in various sectors has been undertaken and published by the Indo-Italian Chamber of Commerce and Industry and PricewaterhouseCoopers[15].

More recently, infrastructure contracts awarded to Italian construction companies such as Enel Green Power, Italferr, Rizzani de Eccher and Astaldi, are a sign of Italy's reawakening interest in India's infrastructure growth.

Indian companies are also playing a decisive role in the future of Italy and Europe's heavy industry and manufacturing sectors: Arcelor Mittal's decisive investment in Taranto's Ilva, the Jindal Group's acquisition of Aferpi steel facilities in Piombino, Titagarh's investment in the Italian railways sector with the acquisition of Firema and the Mahindra Group's acquisition of Pininfarina are clear signs of the growing interest and progressive integration between the two economies.

---

[15] www.indiaitaly.com/IndoItalianNew/Upload/IICCI_PwC_Why_India.pdf

And today? With the Italian marines back in Italy and the Enrica Leixe case transferred to the International Tribunal for the Law of the Sea[16], the diplomatic tensions between Italy and India have ceased to exist. On the contrary, there is an intense agenda of bilateral meetings and visits by institutional representatives of both countries, identifying areas and sectors for collaboration and joint projects[17].

In addition, estimates for bilateral trade indicated promising figures for 2018, with total trade between Italy and India of approximately €9.5 billion, so the projected increase of commercial flows should register a whopping +10%.

The opportunities offered by the Indian market are self-evident. Yet India's great complexity and diversity require a selective and mid-to-long-term engagement, to allow groups of Italian companies, associations, educational institutes and public bodies to identify specific areas upon which focused and scalable projects can be built.

It would be advisable to adopt a granular, sector and state-specific strategy, matching the needs and dimensions of clusters of Italian companies with the requirements of the local stakeholders.

To do this, a coordinated strategy including all the relevant and concerned stakeholders is required: Italian regions, diplomatic representations in India, trade associations, agencies and bilateral chambers of commerce, banking and financial institutions, universities, scientific, cultural and research centres should work in conjunction to effectively implement a concerted strategic plan for India.

To this end, the recent establishment of a strategic think tank by the Italian Ministry of Foreign Affairs and international

---

[16] For the complete dossier of the case, consult Internal Tribunal for the Law of the Sea, Case no. 24.

[17] Italy's Prime Minister Giuseppe Conte visited India in October on the occasion of the India-Italy Tech Summit, Ministry of External Affairs, Government of India, Media Center, *India-Italy Joint Statement during visit of Prime Minister of Italy to India (October 30, 2018)*.

Cooperation along with the Italian Ministry of Economic Development is a promising first step. Bringing together Italian institutional players at a central and regional level, sector and business associations, financial and banking institutions, universities and research centres, the strategic think tank has defined a roadmap for Italy in India, and a series of recommendations, along with a set of proposed projects, have been produced[18].

Italy as a unique ecosystem

As in many parts of the world, Italy is recognised in India for its brands in the fashion, furniture, food & wine and motor sectors. It is also known for its outstanding landscapes, its unparalleled architectural and artistic heritage, its great variety of wine & food traditions. Indeed, as far as quality of life and products are concerned, Italy is foremost in Indians' minds.

What is less known in India is that behind a suit, an armchair, a sports car, or a bottle of wine made in Italy, there is extremely advanced and sophisticated manufacturing knowhow and technological expertise, which has been refined and improved through generations, and that has allowed Italy to become the second biggest manufacturer in Europe and the fifth in the world.

It is the so-called Italian industrial cluster model: a unique ecosystem, based on collaborations among SMEs, artisans, universities and professional education institutes active in the same value-chain, operating within the same territory and tightly integrated. The "Industrial Cluster" can be defined as:

> A productive system based on an agglomeration of enterprises, normally small and medium sized, characterized by a tendency to be tightly integrated both horizontally and vertically and to be highly specialized. They are typically concentrated in a specific territory and bound by a common historic, social, economic and cultural background. [...] One of the most important elements of industrial clusters is the concept of 'industrial atmosphere':

---

[18] Tavolo Riflessione Strategica MAE 2019.

when in a specific territory there is a high number of people doing similar jobs, the "mysteries of that industry are no longer such. It is as if they are in the air, and the kids learn them almost inadvertently[19].

It is thanks to this model that once small, family-run companies operating out of simple workshops and investing in R&D and technology, have turned into the iconic multinational brands and corporations known today by everyone.

Moreover, Italy has been an important area for the birth and prosperity of many civilisations: Greeks, Romans, Arabs, Germans, Dacians and Sarmatians all settled in Italy and left extraordinary traces; in Italy the phenomenon of city-states, which would shape much of European history and topography, first took shape; Italy has been the cradle of Christianity, Humanism and the Renaissance: it harbours within its religious and civil monuments some of the highest achievements of human creativity and thought: it is not surprising, therefore, that Italy boasts the largest number of sites registered in UNESCO's World Heritage Lists.

It also has one of the most biodiverse environments[20], due to its peculiar and favourable geoclimatic features, which allows for a proliferation of ecological niches in very close proximity but highly diversified. A case in point: with 450 registered autochthonous wine grapes (estimates indicate that at least 500 additional varieties have yet to be registered), Italy features the highest variety worldwide.

---

[19] Distretto industriale, translation by the author. In Italy, the industrial clusters have been given institutional identity with Law 317/1991. For more info on the Italian industrial clusters, see Banca Intesa San Paolo latest report: *Economia e finanza dei distretti industriali*, Presentation 10th Annual Report, Direzione Studi e Ricerche, Milan, 29 March 2018.
[20] With 8195 species and subspecies being mapped, Italy is the first country in Europe for autochthonous flora. Source: Plants Biosystems

Organise the community of Italics in India

This extremely varied cultural and natural heritage has translated into an innumerable series of different habits, customs, rituals, festivities, each accompanied by very specific and established wine & food traditions. It is a great cultural and natural wealth, which attracts an ever-growing number of tourists to Italy (amongst them, Indians are growing faster and faster).

It also defines a set of values shared and embraced by a growing community of people called the *Italics*:

> Italics are not just Italian citizens in Italy and abroad. They are, above all, the people of Canton Ticino, Dalmatia, and San Marino, and their descendants; Italian-Americans, those of the two Americas and of Australia; as well as Italian speakers and all those people who might not have a drop of Italian blood in their veins, but have nonetheless embraced our county's values, lifestyle, and shared behavioural models. We estimate that we are talking about approximately 250 million people[21].

It is of crucial importance to communicate this complex and distinct set of features that summarise Italy to the Italics in India. It is equally important to organise this community and their demand for Italian products around a set of promotional activities, aimed at both creating awareness about Italy and its know-how amongst Indians and generating business opportunities for Italian companies and their Indian counterparts.

Sector-specific projects for clusters of companies

The community of Italics in India should be stimulated, engaged and developed through the organisation and implementation of multi-year and multi-stakeholder projects. At the same time, Italian and Indian SMEs should make use of a set of services combining traditional promotional activities (organisation of conferences, seminars, technical round-tables, participation in

---

[21] P. Bassetti, *Let's Wake Up, Italics! – Manifesto for a Glocal Future*, John D. Calandra Italian-American Institute, 2017.

fairs and exhibitions, business delegations, B2B and B2G meetings) and innovative ones (digital, sector-focused promotions, training and education, certification of people and of processes), which are tailor-made for groups of companies and are executed over an extended period of time in as many Indian cities as possible. This can truly facilitate the "soft-landing" of Italian SMEs on the Indian market. These projects should focus on sectors in which Indian demand is particularly high and where Italy can offer know-how, technology, products and services: food & wine, furniture & design; style & fashion; engineering for manufacturing, urban planning for smart & sustainable cities; wellness & healthcare; the entire agro-industrial sector (from farm mechanisation to cold-chain to food processing & packaging).

At the same time, a marketing plan able to ensure continuous recall of brand-Italia in tier I and tier II Indian cities should be implemented.

An effective way to do this is to identify a series of "outposts" where Italian products and technologies can be showcased and promoted and B2B and B2C activities can be organised: these outposts could be either corners within retail outlets or learning centres within universities or technical institutes.

Higher education and vocational training would also play an important role: the demand in India to acquire skills and knowledge from renowned Italian universities and institutes is very high, and trainees can easily become active promoters of Italian products, technologies and know-how. As a marketing and community-building tool, it would be interesting to introduce and launch on the market a series of certification schemes, recognising the competence and experience of promoters of Italian products, know-how and culture in India and elsewhere. The final dream? To build a human-centric, smart & sustainable Italian city in India.

The moment seems to be a very fit one: in 2019, Italy and the world celebrate the five-hundred years since the death of Leonardo da Vinci, one of the Italic multi-disciplinary geniuses whose activity spanned architecture, engineering, defence systems, painting, drawing… and much more. In the next few years, other major Italic personalities who greatly contributed to the history of Italy and of humankind, will be celebrated: Raffaello Sanzio, painter, conservationist and urban planner; Dante Alighieri, the "father" of the Italian language, poet, philosopher and theologian. These are exceptional occasions, offering an outstanding opportunity to convey the values embodied in the idea of Italy worldwide.

Conclusion

The gravitational centre of global geopolitics is progressively shifting towards Asia, due to the demographic and economic prowess of China and India: the Belt and Road Initiative on one side and the Indo-Pacific partnership on the other are two important examples of the assertiveness of the two regions.

Against this backdrop, the European Union finds itself pushed to reiterate and insist on its leadership and experience in the circular economy and smart & sustainable technologies.

Within this context, and after overcoming the diplomatic tensions and revamping its commercial and industrial tie-ups with India, Italy can make use of two outstanding values no other country can: the Made-in-Italy brand, and the concept of Italian lifestyle can be powerful tools to establish and develop in India a community of Italics, people passionate about Italy and its culture, thus organising the demand for Italian products in the country. This community must be kept engaged through a series of sector-specific projects, pooling and bringing together clusters of Italian SMEs, executed over an extended period of time, so as to facilitate the establishment of business collaborations with Indian counterparts. At the same time, these initiatives should make use of a network of outposts, where Italian products, know-how and technologies can be showcased and utilised, also for training purposes.

The celebrations of outstanding Italian personalities such as Leonardo da Vinci, Raffaello Sanzio, and Dante Alighieri

178 India's Global Challenge

should become exceptional arguments to convey the values embodied in the idea of *Italy*, *Made-in-Italy* and the *Vivere all'Italiana* – *The Italian Way of Life*. Such an endeavour requires a joint effort by all the stakeholders: actors of *Sistema Italia* in Italy and India.

The Authors

Antonio Armellini is a diplomat. He was spokesman for Altiero Spinelli and worked with Aldo Moro at the Italian Minister of Foreign Affairs and the Presidency of the Council of Ministers. In addition to performing various assignments abroad and in Italy, he was ambassador-at-large at the CSCE, ambassador to Algeria, India, and Nepal, Permanent Representative to the OECD, and Head of the Italian Mission in Iraq. He is a columnist at Corriere della Sera and he also writes for the Huffington Post, ISPI, and a number international political magazines and newspapers. His books include: *L'elefante ha messo le ali – l'India del XXI Secolo* (2008 and 2013), published in English as *If the Elephant Flies* (2012) and *Né Centauro né Chimera – Modesta Proposta per un'Europa Plurale* (with G. Mombelli, 2016). He is a member of the International Institute of Strategic Studies (IISS, London), the Istituto Affari Internazionali (IAI, Rome), and the Advisory Board of the Official Monetary and Financial Institutions Forum (OMFIF, London).

Gautam Chikermane is Vice President at Observer Research Foundation. His areas of research are Indian and international economic policy, with particular focus on the G20 and BRICS economies. He is also a Director at CARE India. Earlier, he was New Media Director at Reliance Industries Ltd and has served in leadership positions at some of India's largest newspapers and magazines – Hindustan Times, The Indian Express, The Financial Express, and Outlook Money. A Jeffersen Fellow at the East-West Center (Fall 2001), he has authored four books: *70 Policies that Shaped India: 1947 to 2017, Independence to $2.5 Trillion* (2018); *Tunnel of Varanavat* (2016); *The Disrupter: Arvind Kejriwal and the Audacious Rise of the Aam Aadmi* (2014); and *Five Decades of Decay* (1997). A student of India's greatest epic, The Mahabharata, and Dhrupad classical music, he lives in New Delhi and Pondicherry.

Bidisha Ganguly is Chief Economist at the Confederation of Indian Industry (CII), India's premier industry institution. Heading a team of economists and specialists, she is responsible for the economic policy and research work of the Confederation. Her work includes strategic analysis of global and Indian macroeconomic developments and sectoral trends for industry members and interacting with a wide range of stakeholders such as Government, industry, and academia. As Chief Economist, Bidisha represents industry perspectives and coordinates with various stakeholders such as multilateral institutions, global investors, the media and parliamentarians. She is responsible for the publication of a monthly journal Economy Matters which tracks economic developments and provides analysis of important policy issues by subject experts.

Nicola Missaglia is ISPI's Online Publications Manager, as well as a Research Fellow at ISPI's Asia Centre, in charge of the India Desk. Before joining ISPI, he has served for several years as the Scientific Coordinator and Managing Editor for the international think tank Reset-Dialogues on Civilizations. He holds a BA in Philosophy and a Research Master's degree in Political Theory and Contemporary History from Sciences Po Paris Doctoral School (France). As a member of the International Association of Journalists (Brussels), he contributes to Italian and international magazines. He also takes part in research projects commissioned by the Italian Parliament and Ministry of Foreign Affairs.

Abhijit Iyer-Mitra is senior fellow at the Institute of Peace & Conflict Studies. A defence economist, he has regular columns in the economic times & business standard, as well as bylines in all the major national dailies. He is also the author of two books. Prior to this he coordinated the national security programme at ORF, and was visiting scholar at Sandia National Laboratories & the Stimson Centre.

Claudio Maffioletti earned a Postgraduate Diploma in Management at City University – Cass Business School, London, UK. Upon his return to Italy from the UK, he was appointed as General Services Manager at ISPI. He moved to Mumbai, India in 2007, as a General Manager of the Indo-Italian Chamber of Commerce and Industry (IICCI), where he was in charge of the Business Assistance, Operations and Financial Control divisions. He is the Chief Executive Officer and Secretary General of the IICCI since 2015.

Ugo Tramballi is ISPI Senior Advisor in charge of the Institute's India Desk. He is an editorialist for *Il Sole 24 Ore*, a member of the Institute for International Affairs, of the Italian Centre for Peace in the Middle East, and Media Leader at the World Economic Forum. He was a correspondent in the Middle East and in Moscow for *Il Giornale* and a global correspondent for *Il Sole 24 Ore*. He won the Premiolino 1987, Premio Colombe d'Oro per la Pace 2003, Premio Max David 2005, Premio Barzini 2008. Among his writings: *L'Ulivo e le pietre: racconto di una terra divisa* (2002), *Israele: il sogno incompiuto* (2008), *India. The Modi Factor* (with N. Missaglia, 2017), *Mother India* (2019). His blog, Slow News, is dedicated to international events.

Christian Wagner is Senior Fellow at the German Institute for International and Security Affairs (SWP) in Berlin. He held various academic position at universities and think tanks in Germany before he joined SWP in 2003. From 2007 to

2013 he was member of the board of directors of the German Association for Asian Studies (DGA). In 2015/16 he was a Visiting Fellow at the Observer Research Foundation (ORF), the Jawaharlal Nehru Institute for Advanced Studies (JNIAS) and at the Institute for Defence Studies and Analyses (IDSA) in New Delhi. At present he is a member of the International Research Committee (IRC) of the Regional Centre for Strategic Studies (RCSS) in Colombo. His main areas of interest are India and South Asia with a special focus on foreign policy and security issues.

www.ingramcontent.com/pod-product-compliance
Lightning Source LLC
Chambersburg PA
CBHW060454280326
41933CB00014B/2755